AF722336

Theory and Empirics of Economics in the Current Perspective

Theory and Empirics of Economics in the Current Perspective

Edited by
Debnarayan Sarker

Centre for Economics Studies
Department of Economics
Presidency University, Kolkata

ALLIED PUBLISHERS PVT LTD.

New Delhi • Mumbai • Kolkata • Lucknow • Chennai
Nagpur • Bangalore • Hyderabad • Ahmedabad

ALLIED PUBLISHERS PRIVATE LIMITED

D-5, Sector-2, **Noida**–201 301
Ph. Nos.: 0120-4320295/2542557/4352866 • E-mail: delhi.books@alliedpublishers.com

17 Chittaranjan Avenue, **Kolkata**–700072
Ph.: 033-22129618 • E-mail: cal.books@alliedpublishers.com

15 J.N. Heredia Marg, Ballard Estate, **Mumbai**–400001
Ph.: 022-42126969 • E-mail: mumbai.books@alliedpublishers.com

No. 25/10 Commander-in-Chief Road, Ethiraj Lane (Next to Post Office) Egmore, **Chennai**–600008
Ph.: 044-28223938 • E-mail: chennai.books@alliedpublishers.com

P.B No. 9932, No. 15, 3rd Floor (Next to Vijaya Bank), 5th Cross, Gandhinagar, Karnataka, **Bangalore**–560009
Ph.: 080-41530285 / 22386239
• E-mail: bngl.journals@alliedpublishers.com / apsabng@airtelmail.in

Sri Jayalakshmi Nilayam, No. 3-4-510, 3rd Floor (Above More Super Market) Barkatpura, **Hyderabad**–500027
Ph.: 040-27551811, 040-27551812 • E-mail: hyd.books@alliedpublishers.com

Website: www.alliedpublishers.com

First Published: 2011
© 2011, Debnarayan Sarker

No part of the material protected by this copyright notice may be reproduced or utilized in any form or by any means, electronic or mechanical including photocopying, recording or by any information storage and retrieval system, without prior written permission from the copyright owners.

ISBN: 978-81-8424-677-3

Foreword

Theory helps because what we really need is to make an assumption, and theory tells us what the right assumption would be. But the bigger challenge to theory in development economics is to locate the empirical results within a broader intellectual context so that it might not only look to the requirements of economic growth but also to those of a social order based on a welfare state and socialist ideas. As development economics is increasingly becoming an empirical discipline today, the empirical works should not merely intend increasing the national income or accelerating the rate of economic growth, it should take into account the egalitarian and welfare impulses associated with redistribution of income and wealth. What constitutes a balance will vary according to the needs and circumstances of the economy, but given the acceptance on the part of the community of the essential values and ends to be pursued, the empirical works should follow the relevant theoretical underpinnings. This book **Theory and Empirics of Economics in the Current Perspective** is an important attempt dealing with a lot of vital issues in this perspective.

It is my great privilege that I have this opportunity to express my sincere thanks to the contributors who include eminent economists as well as teachers, research fellows and students. My special appreciation and thanks are due to Professor Debnarayan Sarker, the Editor of the collection and Secretary, Centre for Economic Studies, Department of Economics, Presidency University, Kolkata, whose untiring enthusiasm has made the publication of this collection possible.

Prof. Amita Chatterjee
Vice Chancellor,
Presidency University, Kolkata

Preface

The balance between theory and empirics is an ongoing process. No doubt, the pendulum will swing this way and that, and each swing will bring about its own correction. The balance will tend to be restored. This is true in all branches of economics in general and for development economics in particular. But, more importantly, development economics is increasingly becoming an empirical discipline today-it has witnessed an upsurge in innovative empirical research in particular. Fifteen years ago, there was clearly too little empirical work in development economics that met the current frontier standards in establishing inference. Fifteen years on, as the fruits of this empirical excursion have begun to be gathered relating to the problem of accounting for the observed pattern across countries and across time, there is equally a need for theoretical perspective to make the best use of the empirical results in which mathematical techniques are as used in theoretical as in empirical economics, and to continue working on unresolved theoretical issues. However, the primary research concerns in the current perspectives have become increasingly driven by empirical and policy issues. Although there is a marked variations relating to the observed pattern across countries, even across regions within a country, the most important issues of the theory and empirics of economics of every country during the current years is to examine, among others, the inter-relationships among the movements in the output, employment, capital stock, inflation, economic growth, fiscal and monetary policies, business cycles, institutions, environmental problems, on the one hand, and on the other to explain their movements in the distribution of income among the factors of production taking into account the indicators of "physical quality of life" or "human development" issues. This volume has tried to highlight a lot of these vital issues, particularly, in the context of growing economy. All these issues would provide invaluable insights for academics, students, researchers, practitioners and policy makers interested in development, in addition of being a book of teaching students particularly for macroeconomics, development economics and political economy.

The editors takes this opportunity to thank profusely all the contributing authors of this volume. More importantly, this volume comes out through the patronage of the University Grants Commission, and I express my deep gratitude to them. I wish to express my gratitude to Professor Amitava Chatterjee, Head of this department, and Professor Asis Dasgupta who have inspired me greatly to build up this volume. I would like to thank my students, namely, Ismeet Sondhi, Ankita Mitra, Sonak Thakur, Senjuti Ghosh, Sudipta Ghosh and my colleague, Debabrata Lahiri, for helping me in transcribing some important lectures. I am particularly thankful to the non-teaching and library staff of our department, namely Sri Swapan Kumar Das, Sri Subrata Das, Ms. Rita Das, Imam Rasul, Sri Balmiki Prasad and Sri Sankar Hela.

Thanks are due to the publisher of this volume, Allied Publishers, and their staff that helped to put it together.

Debnarayan Sarker
Centre for Economic Studies,
Department of Economics
Presidency University, Kolkata

Contributors

Dr. Amita Chatterjee
Vice Chancellor, Presidency University, Kolkata

Dr. Montek Singh Ahluwalia
Deputy Chairman, Planning Commission of India

Dr. Isher Judge Ahluwalia
Chairman, ICRIER, New Delhi

Dr. Partha Sen
Director, Delhi School of Economics

Dr. Mihir Kanti Rakshit
Professor and Director of Monetary Research Project, ICRA

Dr. Sugata Marjit
Director, Centre for Studies in Social Science, Kolkata and R.B.I. Professor of Industrial Economics

Dr. Abhirup Sarkar
Professor of Economics, Indian Statistical Institute, Kolkata

Dr. Debnarayan Sarker
Professor and Secretary, Centre for Economic Studies, Presidency University, Kolkata

Dr. Rajnarayan Gupta
Associate Professor, Department of Economics, Presidency University, Kolkata

Debabrata Lahiri
Assistant Professor, Department of Economics, Presidency University, Kolkata

Dr. Mousumi Dutta
Associate Professor, Department of Economics, Presidency University, Kolkata

Dr. Zakir Husain
Associate Professor, Institute of Economic Growth, New Delhi

Ankita Mitra
Student, 2nd Year, Department of Economics, Presidency University, Kolkata

Ismeet Sondhi
Student, 2nd Year, Department of Economics, Presidency University, Kolkata.

Shilpi Mukherjee
Student, 2nd Year, Department of Economics, Presidency University, Kolkata

Pratanu Mitra
Student, 3rd Year, Department of Economics, Presidency University, Kolkata.

Srijita Ghosh
Student, 3rd Year, Department of Economics, Presidency University, Kolkata.

Adway De
Student, 3rd Year, Department of Economics, Presidency University, Kolkata.

Puja Kankrania
Student, 3rd Year, Department of Economics, Presidency University, Kolkata.

Aparajita Dasgupta
M.Sc. Applied Economics, Presidency University, Kolkata

Debraj Das
Senior Research Fellow, Centre for Economic Studies, Presidency University, Kolkata

Indrani Basu
Senior Research Fellow, Centre for Economic Studies, Presidency University, Kolkata

Contents

Introduction

Debnarayan Sarker

This volume brings together four selected papers in Section I, presented in the conference at the Centre for Economic Studies (CES), four selected papers in Section II contributed by faculty members and research fellows under the Department of Economics, Presidency University, Kolkata, four selected papers in Section III contributed almost by students who presented those papers in different seminars at the CES, and three reports in Section IV prepared on the discussions of important topics presented in the conference at the CES. All the selected papers cover the most debatable issues on development perspective in general and developing economics in particular together with broad surveys of the literature and suggest concrete ideas for future research.

The first paper on Section I opens with Montek Singh Ahluwalia's paper on 'Theory and Empirics of Economics in dealing with Growth, Inequality and Distribution in India'. He divides his paper into two sections: in the first section he makes some general comments on the issue of the relationship between theory and empirics, and in the second section he addresses as to how these issues have displayed in India dealing very much with growth, inequality and distribution. While examining the relationship between theory and empirics in economics he argues that economics is a policy oriented science. Most people who study economics do not actually study it to understand the world, actually study it to change the world in whatever direction they want. So, one can think of a purely theoretical attempt to explain what is happening, not too much bothered by the desire to change and that's typically what sociology is doing. As regards the growth issue is concerned, he says "we are not only talking about growth, we were talking about inclusive growth and I have no hesitation in saying that while I think we have done extremely well in growth front, it is a correct assessment that we have not done as well as we wanted to or we would like to on the inclusiveness front". These include things like access to health, malnutrition, the quality of education that people have and these issues become very important to find out whether the growth process will be equalizing. Also there is, he argues, unleashing lot of productive potential in organized sector, and the hope was we will bring people from the unorganized sector to the organized sector; however that's the area where the performance has not been as good as it should have been and one of the reasons for that we do not really have a good enough system to spread education and skills very broadly throughout the country.

While examining the critical areas for necessary interventions he said 'we also need to recognize that there are market failures; but there is very significance state failure'. I think the current concern about corruption, slothful bureaucracy, lack of accountability reflect a persuasive feeling. A lot of the answer to it does lie in creating political accountability of the executive at the relevant political level. Other important areas which need to be looked into is that there is huge difference across the country; many of the schemes are working very well in some parts of the country and not working in some parts of the country at all. All of that needs to be carefully built into the development strategy if we want to have the best sense of inclusiveness. However, in fine, he is of the view that we are at the stage where transformation process is benefiting some groups and hurting a large number of other groups. And how to be able to achieve this transformation without too much damage is a difficult and complex task.

In her paper titled 'The Way of Rapid Urbanization: A Major Challenge to India's Development' Isher Judge Ahluwalia provides a critical review of the problems and prospects of India's urbanisation. Urbanization is expected to gather momentum in the years to come, she says, as the Indian economy resumes its journey towards 9-10 per cent per annum growth of GDP, although there has been some apparent slowing down of the growth of urban population in the 1980s and 1990s. She argues that the urban rural divide is a political construct and it can only be erased through bold brushes of development. Policy can play an important role in generating urban-rural synergy. Where will the resources come from for urban infrastructure investment requirements? The important sources, she opines, might be the Municipal Bond market and Public Private Partnership. Also, as cities expand and new cities are developed, special care will have to be taken to ensure that there is room for economically weaker sections and resources for upgrading of slums' land issue. Land use is a major challenge. Town planning schemes of Gujarat, Magarpatta in Pune are the examples where the farmers have come together and formed a development company to urbanize their farm lands. She is in the firm belief that the larger challenge of coordinated city planning encompassing the needs of housing and transport in synergy with the demands arising from rapid economic growth and the need to preserve the environment, is staring us in the face. Capacity building can also be promoted by twinning programs, among cities in the country as well as with international cities. "While the challenges are huge", she says, "I am absolutely confident that we are very close to the tipping point of an urban revolution in India, which, if planned properly, can drive economic growth and be inclusive".

Partha Sen's paper (Monetary Policy in India since Liberalization: The Constraints posed by Fiscal Policy and Capital Flows) critically examines what globalization really means. Is it an unmixed blessings or does it bear with some costs? Why are capital flows, in particular, more significant in that context? The overwhelming experience of globalization is that those who have kept a lid on their capital account and loosened their current account could use globalization successfully. In India if there is so much disquiet over international trade, he thinks, it is because the redistribution has not taken place, and if redistribution takes place then everyone can become better off through trade. If trade in goods is welfare improving (assuming a redistributive policy in place) why isn't trade in financial assets treated at par? Liberalization for India has proved a lot of wrong signals. Many of us, he argues, believed that if we liberalized the manufacturing would get wiped out. But that has not happened. Indian manufacturing has shown a lot of resilience. But the reality is not encouraging: although there have been too much capital flow, there appears too little infrastructure building and too little human capital formation. Fiscal deficit is too high. We have not been privatizing enough. Structural transformation is a non-starter. There is still 60% of population in agriculture. The external sector, the exchange rate, should be the very serious concern in any industrialization strategy. Industrialization is not an unmixed blessing. We have to drag half a million populations or even quarter of a million population out of poverty. What are the environmental cost and things like that? He is of the firm belief that market-oriented way is the true sense of industrialization to pull itself out of poverty, and there we have crippled industrialization by allowing too much of capital inflow.

My paper (Taxation, Income Distribution and Economic Growth in India: Principles, Theory and Empirics) tries to examine the underlying factors influencing the principles of taxation policy of India and to look into its theoretical implications on reality for broader policy framework in Indian perspective. While examining the underlying factors influencing the principles of taxation policy of India, this paper tries to review the structure of Indian economy on four important issues and observes that employment structure has been polarized between a few high-end jobs in large corporations, mostly in service sector, and the mass of low-productive low earning jobs in the unorganized sector that represents the poor, the overwhelming majority of Indian people. A particular policy instrument may be the imposition of tax on capital income (excluding tax on human capital of low-productive low earning jobs) and the government spending on productive services which enhance labor income reflecting thereby to capture the principles of taxation policy of Indian economy—the requirement of Directive Principles of Constitution for social justice together with the leveling down of inequalities and that of positive income growth. But the reality is that indirect tax has been at the cost of basic consumption of the poor and their key distribution issues are at stake.

Rajnarayan Gupta's paper 'Consumerism in India: A Study Based on NSS Data', which appears in Section II, addresses the definitional and measurement problems relating to consumerism. Expenditure on consumer durables and their budget share are considered to be the two indices of consumerism. The study examines the level of consumerism in different states in India. The investigation is made on the basis of NSS (National Sample Survey) data. The report of the 61st round survey of the NSSO (National Sample Survey Organization) has been analyzed for that purpose. The analysis finds wide variation in consumerism across states and across sectors. The variation in consumerism seems to be caused by income inequality in the country.

The fundamental issue of Debabrata Lahiri's paper (Commercial Piracy: Cry for Crackdown and the Issues of Social Surplus) is that in situation where commercial piracy is almost costless technologically, copyright producer's demand for monitoring copyright infringement may vary in intensity depending on factors like market size, the range of vertical differentiation in preference, and deviation in quality of the pirated product from the original version. While the demand of the copyright producer is always for monitoring to ensure monopoly market to her, the social objective may very well warrant a softer attitude to piracy, provided this does not deny her normal profit. .

In our joint paper (Disparity of Manufacturing Industries among Major Indian States: The Importance of Fiscal Reforms during Reform Period) Debraj Das and I make an attempt to present the disparities of state-level performance of manufacturing industry on some key variables and try to examine whether fiscal reforms play a significant role for such a disparity among major Indian states during reform period. The study suggests that Indian states which could contribute to higher economic and administrative reforms during reform period by various fiscal measures did gain the boon of industrial achievements. So, in order to gain industrial uplift, the fiscal reforms of a state has a strong positive impact on increasing income level of the particular state reflecting thereby to develop her economy by receiving the fruits of industrial development.

Mousumi Dutta and Zakir Husain's paper (Crime, Deterrence and Growth in Post Liberalized India: An Application of Seemingly Unrelated Regression Equation Model) attempts to examine the impact of deterrence and socio-economic variables on crime rates in Indian states after the economic liberalization of the 1990s. In particular, they seek to verify whether the theories of crime originating in developed countries are relevant in developing countries. Results of this paper show that economic growth and, in particular, its quality is an important determinant of influencing crime rates. Liberalization of the Indian economy has led to an acceleration of growth; the results of the endogenous model show that this need not reduce crime. This implies that growth process has to be participatory and create opportunities for the entire population in order to control crime rates.

In section III, the first paper starts with our joint paper titled 'The Impact of Inefficient institution on Health in India'. We (Ankita, Ismeet, Shilpi and I) try to examine the effort level by the medical care providers between public medical services and private medical services. While examining the basic issue, this paper points out the main obstacles for healthcare services of public sector in India, the nature of private and public sector healthcare market working in India and the adverse impact on poor by the service of government doctors. The study shows that public doctors exert much less effort and less competence than their private counterparts. It is also observed that both non-MBBS and MBBS exert much less effort in public medical services in relation to their private ones for all types of visit to the patients. In order to examine as to how it is possible to execute such a policy so that both non-MBBS and MBBS may not exert less effort in public medical services in relation to their private one to the patients in different income areas, the analytical theoretical works seem to suggest that in order to help the patients, particularly patients having poor economic condition, government may primarily provide the best incentive scheme to the doctors (equal for same categories of doctors) for their public medical services, but such a incentive scheme should hardly differ from private medical services, if the latter desires to serve. Making public doctors in such areas more responsive to patient needs, this study seems to suggest, may be possible through compensation schemes other than fixed salaries.

Pratanu Mitra's paper (Institutional Issues in Economic Development: A Third World Perspective) tries to examine the impact of coordination failure due to existence of prevalent institutions in a developing owner occupied and rental housing market based on the empirics of a representative city in a developing economy. Institutional constraints are informational constraints, and has human fallibility. Their changes, his study suggests, are difficult, because those institutions have inertia, and they themselves are a result of rigid incentive and hierarchical structures. The changes need shocks to the status quo, something that are political and social. These are institutions with competing incentive structures that have greater acceptance or creditability or power bases.

Adway De, Puja Kankrania and Srijita Ghosh,'s paper (Migration from Informal Urban to Rural Sector: An Approach to Developing Economy) examine the benefit of migration from urban to rural sector for the large number of poor people living in slums in every city. They first try to examine the theoretical underpinnings in analytical forms and then try to justify the same by empirical facts particularly in Indian perspective. They consider two-sector, namely informal urban sector and rural sector, and exclude the analysis of formal urban sector in her theoretical underpinnings. Then migration for an urban individual working in the informal sector is justifiable, they argue, so long as the standard of living of an urban individual working in the urban informal sector having housing accommodation in the rural areas will be equal to the standard of living of a rural individual working in rural sector having housing accommodation within rural sector. From the theory and empirics they conclude that there would possibly an urgent need of an urban-rural migration in India as we have been increasing the process of urbanizing.

In the last paper (Empirics of Development Status in West: An Inter-District Study during 1980-2000) in Section III Aparajita Dasgupta, Indrani Basu and I try to make an assessment of the overall status of development in the state of West Bengal during 1980-2000 with a special stress on the inter-district disparities. The study reveals that district development index is highly influenced by agricultural productivity, employment and infrastructure. The districts which have exhibited good performance, for example, in terms of agricultural composite index have not necessarily shown the same performance in other areas. Districts like Midnapur, Darjiling, Burdwan, Hoogly, 24 parganas (north), Howrah, have shown fairly consistent high ranking in terms of all the composite indices. This paper, however, suggests that the growth of income is not adequate to bring about overall status of development of West Bengal.

Section IV presents three reports based on the critical discussions of three eminent economists, Professor Mihir Kanti Rakshit, Professor Sugata Marjit and Professor Abhirup Sarkar at the national level conference of CES.

This volume, in particular, addresses development issues of growing economics in the current perspective in dealing with growth, inequality and distribution, principles of taxation for the promotion of redistribution of income and economic growth, proper planning for rapid urbanization suited to inclusive growth, the problems and prospect of constraints posed by fiscal policy and capital flows due to liberalization, problems and policies towards efficient institution on health and housing market, the benefit of migration from urban to rural sector for the large number of poor people living in slums in every city, policies towards reducing income inequalities due to variation in consumerism across states and across sectors, strategies for fiscal measures towards industrialization, proper policy measures for socio-economic ills of crimes and the like. Each paper poses a policy question together with appropriate method of analysis, and almost provides empirical examples using appropriate data. This volume also presents reports on the discussion of macroeconomic perception, food price inflation and status driven utility analysis based on conflicting measure of poverty and inadequate savings. The book would provide, due to its contemporariness and comprehensiveness, invaluable insights to policy makers, researchers, academics, practitioners and policy makers interested in development, in addition to being a book of teaching students particularly for macroeconomics, development economics and political economy.

Theory and Empirics of Economics in Dealing with Growth, Inequality and Distribution in India

Montek Singh Ahluwalia*

This—'Theory and Empirics'—is a difficult subject for anyone to talk about particularly in an academic institution. You know all scientific developments really consist of theory being contrasted with empirical facts and then theory develops in the light of that empirical fact. I want to divide my remarks into two sections: first I want to make some general comments on the issue of the relationship between theory and empirics, then I want to address at least in my perception of how these issues have played out in India dealing very much with (the same questions that I think Prof. Sarker has referred to) growth, inequality and distribution in India.

PART I

Relationship between Theory and Empirics in Economics

As far as the central general point about theory and empirics is that one thinks of theory, at least in the social sciences, has to be an explanation of whatever empirical facts interest you. So the purpose of a theory is to try to explain what is happening. I mean, unlike sociology, economics is a policy oriented science. Most people who study economics don't actually study it to understand the world, actually study it to change the world in whatever direction they want. So, you can think of a purely theoretical attempt to explain what is happening, not too much bothered by the desire to change, and that's typically what sociology is doing. Go off and look at primitive societies or contemporary societies and examine them in very great detail: all that is relevant for change, but that's not the principal objective of the study of economics. Most economists, on the other hand, quickly want to do some theory and then build on that theory to make some recommendations on how to accelerate growth, how to bring about

*Speech delivered by Dr. Montek Singh Ahluwalia, Deputy Chairman Planning Commission of India, at the UGC sponsored National Conference of Centre for Economic Studies, Presidency University, Kolkata on August 28, 2010.

faster poverty reduction, better income distribution etc. and I think this creates a little bit of tension, because when you are very keen to push policies you may also attempt to suppress if the theory doesn't fit into your prejudices. That's not to say that you shouldn't do that what one is constantly bearing. I am sure many of you are familiar with the work of Kuhn's "Structure of Scientific Revolutions" where he talks about how theory responds to new empirical developments and it keeps getting redefined to fit the new facts. But then there comes a time when the facts, quite obviously, require the theory itself to be completely recast and you get what Kuhn calls a paradigm shift. It's not just elaborating something simply saying, "well, this is really not the way the world works. We thought it did but it's actually quite different." In economics too these things happen.

I would like to give some simple examples. Suppose you were very concerned about economic growth, and you had a very simple theory that said basically production is a function of capital stock; therefore, the growth is a function of investment, and that's what people used to think way back in the 1940's, Harrod-Domer, etc. All the focus was on investment. If you want growth you do more investment; you have a capital-output ratio that will generate additional output. Over time, people recognize that's a very crude oversimplification of the issue and that output is actually not just a function of capital stock, many other things that are involved with change- technology, labor, the degree of skilled labor. It's not just labor but you have skilled labors: the ability to make the most of the technology that's available. Are you really on the technological frontier? That depends a lot on institutions, market pressure of competition, etc. So if you take the approach then there are many things that are going to affect output, not just investment, and it's quite possible to go through several years just pushing investment and getting no results whatsoever. And I think some of the early works that Isher Judge Ahluwalia did focused on that problem in India when people, hardly, cared about total productivity growth. So I mean I am just giving you an example that depending on how you define the theory you can extract whatever policy conclusion you want.

PART II

The Principles of Growth

As regards the issue of growth is concerned, nobody is actually interested in aggregate growth and you know no policy makers, especially is a democratic country, can fail to recognize that the purpose of going on growth is to create an expanding base, on which you can build a more broadly based growth of income. So income of everybody should be growing and that brings in the question of whether some people are gaining more than others; but it also brings in the question: what is it that determines the distribution of income? If you don't believe that there is some kind of iron law which says that in the early stages of development inequality will widen and later on it will narrow down, and in which case you have to pretty much accept that and counter it as best you can. Interestingly, this was the attitude in Planning Commission in the early '60's. Alternatively, you can take the view that distribution of income depends on the nature of growth that you have. So if you go for a particular kind of growth, may be which does more for agriculture, more for small scale industries, then you will automatically get a more equal distribution; but then the issue arises–how much are you sacrificing in terms of overall growth? So, the question of tradeoff between these things becomes relevant. I'm saying all this simply to lay the foundation whenever we discuss a policy issue in India that has to be some common perception, commonly shared perception of how an economy works, what is the theoretical construct that effectively describes what happens and then within that what is it that you can change. Economics are very concerned about changing and the truth of the matter is that if you think of the instruments of change as policy variable and other things are not policy variables—exogenous variables, behavioral variables and so on to some extent, the results you get on how to change the economy depends first of all on how many policy variables you have and that requires you to model the impact of those variables on the economy. But it may also depend on how richly you describe the rest of the economic system and it is very possible by somewhat more elaborate set of relationships to get quite different results depending on which policy variable(s) you choose. So, I think you should remember always: what is the underlying assumption that somebody is making when they say 'X' will lead to affect 'Y'? Underneath that has to be a particular characterization of the economy; and if you don't agree with the policy conclusion necessarily, you need to try to understand what that is. Otherwise, you just get it's perfectly possible to have economists: one fellow has one characterization of the economy based on which some policy conclusions follow, another has a completely different characterization of the economy-based of which totally different conclusions follow and you have a highly ideological debate on these two policy conclusions. That is actually what the newspapers do and I think that's not what should be done in a university.

India's High Growth Strategy

So, building on this very general statement let me turn to what I think are interesting issues in the way this has evolved in India. Now, you know, accelerating growth is a very long spanning objective which goes well even before independence. In fact it was an alumnus of this college, Netaji Subhas Chandra Bose, who was then President of the Congress Party, set up the National Planning Committee under Pt. Jawaharlal Nehru to sort of to try to (this was back in 1938) ask the question of as and when independence happens, what should be our economic objectives, and that committee never submitted it's report because obviously the war broke out in 1939; but we know from the papers, that were prepared for that committee that has come to the conclusion, that being a poor country the scope for redistributing wealth is actually very limited. If you needed to do something to raise the standard of living of the people then you needed—they didn't call it growth–doubling or trebling of wealth over a ten year period. If you translate it into growth, it says, you should have a growth rate between 7 and 11%, and that was in the pre-war years' growth objective. Later, on the Bombay Plan, which was a bunch of businessmen, they said we must have a growth rate of 6% or so. Then when our planning exercise started with P.C. Mahalanobis playing the leading role (he was actually principal of this college for more than one occasion) for he was very much part of the history of this process and at that time target was set at around 5%. Now a kind of strategy which was investment oriented effected by (I think, Prof Sarker referred to) the Mahalnobis model that was put in place. But the actual results was much below 5%. I mean in the '60's and '70's Indian economy grew at 3%/2%.

Now it is interesting, if you go back, to talk about: what was the reaction of people? Well, there were two sorts of reactions. First reaction was, well, you know 3.5% is much better than pre-independence, because, after all, during pre-independence we stagnate. Even though we are not reaching our target, you cannot say that 3.5% is bad. As a matter of fact, in the early years people felt that they were doing better than in pre-independence years. Another set of reactions was that, well, 3.5% is not very different from what the industrialized countries grew at after the industrial revolution. So, generally a sort of willingness to accept that 5%

is not just feasible, 3.5% is not bad. This began to change when people began to realize that at that low growth you're not going to make a difference to poverty at all. In 1960, two or three, I think, brought out a paper on perspectives of development. Now that paper asked the question the other way round. If you want everybody to reach a minimum standard of living in 15 years really with a base of '60-'61 what is the growth strategy we need to do that by 1970-76? And they came to the conclusion that they need high growth; so, they said that 6% or something like that was necessary. They also recognized that in all probability income distribution would deteriorate in initial stages. But nevertheless if you grow fast and there is a little bit of worsening of income distribution: the income levels of many people would be going up and they came to the conclusion that if the economy grows at 6%, even allowing for the change in income distribution, everybody, except the bottom quintile, would be above the poverty line. So they said, 'well, we have to do something for the bottom quintile'. So it was 1965 growth strategy but doing something for the bottom quintile through targeted programs, special programs are necessary to help themselves who would not make themselves benefitted from the growth. Of course what actually happened came to light in the writings of Ashok Rudra. He wrote a piece, which I think, by saying that let's stop chasing this chimera of growth never going to happen and let's concentrate all our efforts at redistributing and actually helping the poor. Now there is a very key assumption there where he was absolutely right: if we can't do better than 3.5% and had to reduce poverty then definitely we had to do more redistribution. But the question was not asked, 'why are we not doing better than 3.5%? That question began to be asked around the 1980s or so. By then, during the 1960s and 1970s, some East Asian countries—Korea, Taiwan, Singapore, and Hong Kong—did extremely well, but we tended to dismiss their performance for variety of reasons. Korea and Taiwan, because they were American allies, were getting lot of assistance from there. Hong Kong and Singapore, because they were city states, had tendency to ignore this superior type of performance. But you know by the 1970s the East Asian countries also began to do well: Malaysia, Thailand, Indonesia were growing at 6%–7% and that is what led to rethinking in India that we don't just have to accept low growth; we have to ask the question: why is growth low? And that led to a whole issue of what determines growth, what determines productivity, all of which at that time was controversial. A belief, for example, that too much control over the private sectors sends wrong signals and curtails entrepreneurial initiatives. The basic belief that government intervenes on the basis of superior knowledge, whereas the private sector has limited knowledge, I think this assumption, came to be challenged. Obviously, it would be true when government intervenes if its knowledge was vastly greater than individual entrepreneurs. But today actually the view is that because government intervention has to be actually very process based, it is never able to internalize all the information that many dispersed decision makers have. And entrepreneurship consists of pushing an idea and trying to get it done went through a bureaucratic process that idea would never be allowed to surface. So, I think this was the underlying change what determines production and productivity requires many other things, and the excessively controlled economy that we had developed was actually making it difficult for the system to become more efficient. This was controversial then; nevertheless, changes began in 1980s and it was after the crisis of 1991, there was a big burst of reform.

Now it is interesting that when that happened one good thing inspired our society—that's what Amartya sen's "Argumentative Indian" describes it quite well that everything is challenged- and I generally think that's a good thing. When these changes were made, the criticism, that was thrown at those trying to make changes, was that this will be an unmitigated disaster—that industry will collapse; you are opening up the economy's foreign trade, you'll never be able to complete; reducing tariffs that's a terrible idea; you need very high protection for having economic growth and the result will be a collapse of economic growth and impoverishment. Now I can't go into this in detail but the changes were made very gradually, and therefore they took a bit of time to have their full effect. Had they been made faster, the full effect would have come earlier but it may not have been politically possible to mobilize consensus. Nevertheless, I am venturing to suggest that if you look back at what has happened, one statement can categorically be made: the view that India's growth potential cannot reach the high growth rate of East Asian economics was comprehensively wrong. And therefore, any policy conclusion based on that would, in my view, be incorrect. I think that the result shows that before the global crisis for 4 years, the Indian economy grew at 9% in the global crisis. There was a slow down but the growth rate of the economy is still very impressive this year. We are hoping it will be 8.5% at a time when the United States is at 2%, Europe may be even less than 2%. We are actually second only to China in the rate of growth that we are maintaining. So, I think on the growth side of the equation there has been a pretty significant change in the perception that when the government argued for certain changes in policy in the belief that these changes would lead to higher growth, that argument was valid, the analysis was valid, the policy instruments identified to achieve that particular result were valid. But I think we are not only talking about growth, we are also talking about inclusive growth, and I have no hesitation in saying that while I think we have done extremely well in growth front, it is a correct assessment that we have not done well we wanted to or we would like to on the inclusiveness front.

Inclusive Growth and Poverty

I don't believe the kind of extreme statements like growth is there, but the rich have become richer and the poor have become poorer, and poverty has increased. I am persuaded by that, I think, there is no doubt that all the data demonstrate that the percentage of the population below the poverty line is definitely declining. I should mention by the way that the last available data on poverty is for the year 2004-05, the next available data will be for 2009-10. Although NSSO produces consumer services more or less every year—it's only in every 5 year—the consumer services are large enough to give reliable estimates of poverty for the whole country and for the individual states. So official estimates of poverty are based on large sample survey and the last of those was 2004-05. So one important thing to remember is that the results of the period of rapid growth, which actually is from the period 2003-04 to now, and their impact on poverty is not known. The data that we have relates to a prior period, and that still has a good growth period. I think the fact is that growth has led to decline in poverty; but when growth accelerated, the rate of decline in poverty did not accelerate, i.e. between 1993-94 and 2004-05 the growth rate was higher than in the period between 1980's and 1993-94. What the data show is that the decline in poverty per year, the percentage point decline per year, is more or less same. So, in one sense you may say that poverty is declining, but I think you can say and it is a valid critique that although the growth increased, it had less impact on poverty. Of course we don't have the most recent information; so what the impact of last 4-5 years has been, we will know only a couple of years below. But the thing, that is more important now, is to define the concern with poverty to be very different from what happened to poverty below a fixed poverty line. Our poverty line is pretty low and therefore while it is relevant to us whether the percentage below the poverty line went down, many people rightly feel that there are so many other dimensions of poverty which are not captured by this poverty line. They include things like access to health, malnutrition, the quality of education that people have and these issues become very important if you are trying to find out whether the growth process will be equalizing. If you have an economy which is unleashing lot of productive potential in organized sector and the hope is we will bring people from the unorganized sector to the organized sector, that's the area where the performance has not been as good as it should have been. One of the reasons for that we don't really have a good enough system to spread education and skills very broadly throughout the country. In fact, in the last 5 or 6 years, that's been an area where the government now has been giving the maximum attention. It's particularly relevant for rural areas because if you want the rural population to have competitive skills to enable them get the kind of jobs we expect to generate in urban areas, then the quality of rural education has to be a lot better. And even in education, there is improvement in some dimensions, in terms of enrollment, in terms of how many schools there are, even in terms of recruitment of teachers. But it is yet to be translated into good quality of education. It has to be changed if we want to get a better outcome. Another dimension what people often talk about is what has been the growth process across the states. Now there, I think, it can be argued that in the last 6 or 7 years the growth process across the states has become a little bit more equalizing, what used to be called the "bemaru" states – Bihar, Madhya Pradesh, Orissa, U.P. and Rajasthan. These, in earlier stages, did not participate much in growth process but more recent data seem to show that even in these states a growth accumulation has taken place. But on the other hand, there's a new dimension which is now receiving lot of attention and that is even in the better states there are backward regions that are not benefitting at all. The current focus on the problems being faced in those parts of the country which are forested and have a very heavy percentage of schedule tribes' population. How are they being affected by our growth process? This is a new dimension of the last several years which we really do need to grapple with; otherwise we will not achieve the kind of inclusiveness we want.

So, target of inclusiveness or inclusive growth, which is actually a shifting target, is perfectly possible. We did this in the 11th plan. We did a listing, instead of having a growth target, a growth and reduction in poverty target. We have 27 monitorable indicators which would indicate the inclusiveness of growth. So growth of GDP is one of them, growth of states and interregional areas is also another one, reduction in poverty is the third; improvement in the nutrition of children, infant mortality rates, maternal mortality rates, education rates, gender difference in education, is to be narrowed down. So it is a multi-dimensional area of inclusiveness which we are now trying to chase. It has never been the position of the Govt. or any of the policy planner that economic reforms or liberalization, is the removal of the state or the withdrawal of the state from the economy. What it has always meant is the withdrawal of the state from certain activities where it really was not adding value. But what actually obstructed the potential for growth in the economy and its redirection and expansion into those areas which are necessary for intervention, but not enough intervention is taking place. So, what are those areas?

Critical Areas for Necessary Interventions

It is not possible to think that farmers left to what markets in rural areas themselves can achieve a great breakthrough. You need a converted effort in which the government, the central and state, work on provisional infrastructure in rural areas, irrigation research capabilities of the system, bring in the new seed varieties that would be suitable for different areas, build the infrastructure needed for enhanced agricultural output to get to the market. This last part is very crucial because as we move away from food grain dominated agriculture to diversified agriculture, you're getting into products that cannot be stored for a very long period except for getting high quality refrigeration etc. that requires a very different kind of eco. system than in the first stage of the Green Revolution where all you needed was to buy the seed of wheat and store it or buy the paddy or rice and store it. So, all these things require very substantial effort plus, of course, education and health where we are lagging behind. Much more effort by the government is needed and finally infrastructure and development requires coordination, planning, taking an overview, and it now involves a combination of public investment as well as public-private partnership. This last part is relatively new phenomenon. Clearly you need to plan infrastructure. But having planned infrastructure it does not have to be built only by the government. It could be put out an appropriate public-private partnership and given the resource constrains, given the importance of building infrastructure in rural areas where only the government can do it, overview is that wherever possible we should optimize the scope of building infrastructure through public-private partnership. And here again the empirical data suggest that quite a lot can be done. I mean if you look at last 10 years there is no doubt that people who earlier felt that infrastructure cannot be developed except through the public sector, probably now agree that it can be developed by public-private partnership. But there is huge number of problems in how to make sure that public-private partnership does not become a chronic capitalism. In the 11th plan we have made that point saying that public-private partnership is about putting private money to public projects. So how you achieve that depends very much on the regulated framework on which the system works. So thus, some of the theories that come up, as far as the liberalization process is concerned, we need to be sure when the markets are complete and when markets are not complete. When markets are not complete we need a lot of remedial action and not just leave it to the market. Markets, on the other hand, which are incomplete and efficient are better off leaving things to the market and that distinction is not always easy to make and I think one needs to carefully identify where are these market failures. At the same time we also need to recognize that there are market failures and there are state failures. What is it that we can do to prevent state failures? I think the current concern about corruption, slothful bureaucracy, lack of accountability—these all reflect a persuasive feeling. There is very significance state failure; a lot of the answer to it does lie in creating political accountability of the executive at the relevant political level. Under the constitution, principle of decentralization suggests that local elected bodies should hold schools and local health clinics. One of the interesting things is: there is huge difference across the country (the notion that there is an all India average experience is a statistical average): many of the schemes are working very well in some parts of the country and not working in some parts of the country at all. And we have to find out why that is happening and how we can replicate this successful behavior. For example, on education, the southern states end up having a much better performance record than the northern states and yet the constitution is the same, the scheme is the same, the central government is the same. But we need to ask why it is working here and not working there.

One of the features of economic change is that there is going to be structural changes and when you have levels of structural transformation, structural transformation doesn't mean every economic activity will continue at higher of productivity. It does not mean that certain activities will die out. The faster you try to grow, faster is the pace of structural transformation and the faster is the pace in which certain activities simply disappear, and that actually creates a lot of pain. One needs to be able to do something, if certain kind of activities are unviable to people. If people are going to be thrown out of the jobs that's a human problem which cannot be ignored. Therefore, the idea of supporting them in these times of transition is by programs of retaining etc. All of those need to be carefully built into the development strategy if you want to have the best sense of inclusiveness. For the last few years, our system of garbage collection in urban areas have been completely chaotic. Unsegregated garbage dumped somewhere or the other and as a matter of fact an entire economic activity of rag pickers has evolved. Increasingly the cities are now thinking of modernising their garbage collection system. It is more efficient, it's more hygienic, some of it can even be proved to be useful in generating energy, Methane gas is evolved, but in that activity rag picking activity disappears. This brings out the question whether the economy of rag pickers are destroyed. Yes, it is destroyed. In this particular case, the solution has to be that you find ways of bringing this group of people to do some other kind of economic and productive activity.

Concluding Remarks

This is relatively easy to do when large parts of the economy are growing and only a few pockets are affected. We are at the stage of development where transformation process is benefitting some groups and hurting a large number of other groups. And how to be able to achieve this transformation without too much damage is a difficult and complex task. I just mention this because sometimes there is a tendency to think that there is a way of designing growth process without hurting anybody. Ultimately growth happens because productivity increases and certain new technology are drawn, and there are many examples when modern cities have transportation like buses and taxis come, *tangas* disappear, the entire profession disappears. How do you arrange that? From that point of view of someone, who is more familiar with issues of policy and less familiar with issues of theory, I just thought I would share with you how it does look from the point of view of a policy making person.

The Way of Rapid Urbanization: A Major Challenge to India's Development

Isher Judge Ahluwalia*

Much of India still lives in its villages but more and more of it is moving towards cities. In 2010, the urban population of India is conservatively estimated at 350 million, although at 30 per cent of the total population, it is much smaller than in other major developing economies, e.g., China (45 per cent), Indonesia (54 per cent), Mexico (78 per cent), South Korea (82 per cent), and Brazil (87 cent).

There has been some apparent slowing down of the growth of urban population in the 1980s and 1990s, but urbanization is expected to gather momentum in the years to come as the Indian economy resumes its journey towards 9-10 per cent per annum growth of GDP. Some estimates suggest that urban population of India would double to 600 million between 2001 and 2030. I would safely project that India's population in 2030 will be in the neighborhood of 550 million. Considering that a large proportion of the current urban population is hugely inadequately served with basic urban services, rapid urbanization poses a very serious challenge to India's development.

At India's current stage of development, industry and service sectors will be the principal drivers of growth. While investments in water, soil fertility and bio-diversity are essential to strengthen the supply potential of agriculture, and research and its dissemination are crucial to realize the agricultural potential, the pattern of non-agricultural growth will have a significant impact on the rejuvenation of agriculture. As the Indian economy goes through a major structural transformation with increasing share of industry and services, this drives the process of migration to cities as they play an increasing role in sustaining rapid growth in the economy.

After the demonstrated success of IT and BPO sectors, and subsequently of pharmaceuticals and auto-component sectors, more and more industry

*Speech delivered by Dr Isher Judge Ahluwalia, Chairman ICRIER, at the UGC sponsored National Conference of Centre for Economic Studies, Presidency University, Kolkata on August 28, 2010.

and service sectors are preparing for global competitiveness, e.g., healthcare, financial services, steel, cotton textiles, food processing. This creates demand for engineers, managers, doctors, nurses and health management officials. Once the educational system and vocational training are reoriented to create the skills that are in demand, there will be growing employment opportunities in urban areas.

Whether it is through agglomeration economies in existing cities or through location of industry in Industrial Corridors or Special Economic Zones with their implications for new urban settlements, it is clear that cities will play a very important role in the new dynamics of growth. As the agglomeration economies of the cities energize industrial growth in a new competitive environment, there will be synergetic linkages with agriculture.

Policy can play an important role in generating urban-rural synergy. For example, liberalization of investment in modern retail will attract large investments in cold-storage, refrigeration and logistics and thereby encourage high value-added agriculture. Similarly, amendment of the Agriculture Produce and Marketing Act (APMC) by state governments will create a national market for agricultural produce and generate better returns for farmers and better prospects for value-added investments in industry and services.

Cities of India need to be prepared for playing their new role. At present, a large urban system of 5161 cities and towns generates 60 per cent of India's GDP. Not only do the cities need much more by way of basic infrastructure but systems have to be put in place so that effective delivery of basic urban services at affordable prices is made available to all including the poor. As cities expand and new cities are developed, special care will have to be taken to ensure that there is room for economically weaker sections and resources for upgrading of slums.

India's urbanization challenge is compounded by the fact that approximately 65 million persons or 23.6 percent of the total urban population live under conditions of absolute poverty. Slums are the most visible manifestation of inadequate shelter and poverty in the urban areas.[1] In 1991, slums accounted for 21.3 per cent of the total urban population, the absolute number being 46–47 million out of a total urban population of 217.9 million persons. In 2001, the number of slums

[1]Not all slum dwellers are poor. The non-poor live in because rent control laws have precluded the provision of low cost rental housing.

dwellers nationwide, as estimated from a survey of 607 cities, is about 40 million or 14.12 percent of the total urban population. Most of the slum settlements lack water and sanitation systems, and are often located in high risk areas of cities. Environmental degradation now represents one of the most formidable challenges on the productivity of the urban poor.

Since we now expect Indian economy to grow at a rate of 8-10 per cent per annum in the foreseeable future, we should expect that by 2030, 40 per cent of India will be living in urban areas. This shift in demographics will have far reaching economic and political implications for a nation that has been accustomed historically to the concept of living in villages. We need a major change of mindset as we address this urban challenge which is ahead of us.

The abysmally poor state of service delivery in the urban areas across the country is too well known for me to spell out. Whether you look at solid waste management, water supply, waste water treatment, other basic services or affordable housing for the poor, the urban landscape is definitely not befitting the great country that we aspire to be. Seventeen years after the Constitutional Amendment, which asked for specific assignment of functions to urban local bodies, we still have a very diverse and not clear assignment of functions to urban local bodies. What is worse is that funds and functionaries have not been devolved along with functions. Both effective devolution of financial powers and securing the revenue base of municipal corporations is really lacking grossly.

In the committee that I am chairing for the Ministry of Urban Development, we are working on estimates for urban infrastructure investment requirements which will take care of both the backlog and accommodate the requirements of a growing urban population. The study by the McKinsey Global Institute has estimated that India will need one trillion dollars of investment in urban infrastructure between 2011 and 2030. What we need to focus on is where the resources are going to come from. Fiscal transfers from the Federal Government by the Jawaharlal Nehru Urban Renewal Mission are just a drop in the bucket. We need to look at other viable sources of financing and there are only two that come to mind, one is the Municipal Bond market and the other is Public Private Partnership.

It goes without saying that first and foremost, we need to strengthen the revenue base of the Municipalities. Property tax is a major source of revenue for urban local bodies. But we find that at the stroke of a pen, a state Government can take away this revenue from the urban local bodies [ULBs] by lowering the property tax rate, depending on which part of the electoral cycle they are in. We saw this recently in Punjab, Haryana and Rajasthan. What is worse, the urban local bodies were not compensated for this. There is a lot that can be done by the urban local bodies themselves to improve the system of assessment and widen the coverage of the tax which forms an important part of their own revenue. Improvement in governance will go a long way to realize the potential of this tax.

Of course, the ULBs have to address the question of user charges for water and sewerage. Considering that for a long time consumers have regarded the supply of water as a free commodity, this has created a situation in which poor pricing rules and worsening governance has led to lack of investment and maintenance in the systems which are responsible for the delivery of these basic services. User charges for water and sewerage have to be linked with improvement in governance including improvement in financial practices, accounting practices, and timely audit of the accounts.

It is important to recognize that avenues such as the Municipal bond market and Public Private Partnerships cannot be tapped unless there is improvement in the internal revenue generation capacity – present and/or future, of the Urban Local Body. Unfortunately, the soft option provided by the Jawaharlal Nehru Urban Renewal Mission has meant that some municipalities which were accessing the market for bonds and some small municipalities which were even coming together to pool and tap the market, now have a soft option in the form of grants from the Government of India.

As for Public Private Partnership, again, you need a revenue model which inspires confidence in the public partner, on the one hand, and the capacity at the ground level on the part of the Urban Local bodies to structure these partnerships, on the other. We need to build this capacity. There is a Public Private Partnership cell in the Finance Ministry but that has the responsibility for infrastructure of all sorts. Perhaps, we need a special Public Private Partnership Cell for Urban Infrastructure which trains the Municipal Commissioners and others on how to enter into Public Private Partnership with proper risk assignment. Take the example of the metro city of Manila, where in converting non revenue water into water, the government divided the city of Manila into two parts, and both halves entered into PPPs: one partnership was extremely successful and the other one collapsed mainly because they had not covered foreign exchange risk. They did not expect the Asian financial crisis, which became their undoing. Also, the private sector would come in, only if there is accountability and transparency. This is possible with greater involvement of civil society and guidance from state and central governments.

The Jawaharlal Nehru Urban Renewal Mission is a good first step which has helped to focus the mind on the urban problem. However, it is too little, too late, and too soft. We need to improve the design of the Jawaharlal Nehru Urban Renewal Mission and expand its scope, but it would still be a small drop in a big bucket. We need to tap these other sources that I have just mentioned. No matter how you approach it, in the end, it boils down to Governance.

Having said that, in the course of our Committee's work, we have been travelling all over the country and what we find is a new dynamism among Municipal Commissioners and Urban Local Body Managers. They are enthused by some of the best practices that are happening in some ULBs in India and they want to emulate these best practices and adapt them, but they don't know how to go about it. For example, by reforming its Property Tax Regime, Bangalore has been able to increase its revenue by 65% by going in for GIS, area based valuation and online payment of taxes. There are other heartening examples like 24/7 water in three cities of Karnataka, the sanitary landfill in Gorai, the bus transport service in Indore and public-private-citizen partnership in Alandur to provide 100 per cent sewerage network and also partial treatment of waste water. You don't have to go very far to look for solutions as you can learn from experience within the country.

We need to create enabling conditions. There is a great deal of work that needs to be done to orchestrate the interface of urban local bodies with civil society. There is an imperative need for political will to cut through corruption and generate accountability. Above all, there is need for leadership.

Let me now turn to the land issue. This is a major challenge. When it comes to expanding the existing towns as the pressures of urbanization increase, we have some models, e.g., town planning schemes of Gujarat which unlock land value and use the funds to create infrastructure for the expansion of the town, and/or Magarpatta in Pune, where the farmers have come together and formed a development company to urbanize their farm lands.

The town planning scheme in Gujarat is based on the original Bombay Act. In Gujarat, they have made amendments so that they could bypass the Land Acquisition Act. They had many cases where while planning the town expansion, they have taken the surrounding areas, had an engagement with the public, taken the stakeholders into confidence in providing for infrastructure. If a road has to go through a plot x, every landowner in the town has to squeeze to make room for the road. The owner of plot x is next to the road with a somewhat smaller plot, and everyone else's plot is similarly reduced. This means that all stakeholders in this expanded area reap the benefit of the new infrastructure. Individual landowners will see their holding proportionally reduced as land is reclaimed by the Government for infrastructure but this is more than offset by the enormous increase in the valuation of the land remaining with them. Maharashtra has not done this. Similarly, for Mumbai, we need to look at urban infrastructure in an integrated manner. The Remaking Mumbai Federation is looking at how parts of inner city Mumbai can be rejuvenated. If you are going to need the services of the poor, you have to ensure basic amenities to the labor force.

More generally, urban planning should not be limited to land use planning. The larger challenge of coordinated city planning encompassing the needs of housing and transport in synergy with the demands arising from rapid economic growth and the need to preserve the environment, is staring us in the face. If India is to grow at 8-9 per cent per annum in the coming decades, as seems more and more likely, cities will have to be the engines of growth which will drive innovation in the midst of agglomeration economies. Urban planning will have to ensure that the congestion diseconomies are kept in check.

I believe that the urban rural divide is a political construct and it can only be erased through bold brushes of development. Urban planning is an important function in bridging the urban rural divide. This function must be carefully looked at by both the State and local governments – at a State level for intercity/inter district linkages, and at the city level for town planning activities. At times planning cuts across many States, as in the case of the Delhi Mumbai Industrial Corridor.

Building the soft infrastructure is critical for execution on the ground. The JNURM experience has shown that there is not enough absorptive capacity at the ULB level. Just providing finances will end up being a case of good money down the drains. Thus, while the investment needs set out by McKinsey and HPEC need to be financed, it must be phased out (a big bang approach may not work) to cater to the current skill deficits at the ULBs.

The capacity building thrust can be in the form of new educational institutions, creation of dedicated municipal cadres or putting in place interdisciplinary mobile teams that cater to a cluster of local bodies. Capacity building can also be promoted by twinning programs, among cities in the country as well as with international cities.

While the challenges are huge, I am absolutely confident that we are very close to the tipping point of an urban revolution in India, which if planned properly can drive economic growth and be inclusive.

Monetary Policy in India since Liberalization: The Constraints posed by Fiscal Policy and Capital Flows

Partha Sen*

In India there is lot of talk and we do not seem to be progressing much beyond talk in academic circle about the merits of and losses from globalization. I am not particularly fond of the word globalization. It is not clear if we call it globalization if we listen to western music or wear western clothes. But let's take it at its face value and say integration with the rest of the world is globalization. There is a lot of talk, lot of bickering and differences of opinions on the issue of what happens to any developing country like India which was pursuing an inward-looking strategy when it opens up to the influences of the rest of the world. The question is: what is it that globalization is supposed to do? Is it an unmixed blessings or can it come with some costs? Why are capital flows, in particular, more significant in that context? Most mainstream economists would feel that international trade in goods is a good thing. I think the mainstream economists also go a little overboard on that. Basically the idea is: if I can produce something which has a higher price in the world market then I should be allowed to export that; if he can import something from the rest of the world at a cheaper price why should he be producing that at home? So trade in goods is in some sense welfare improving. The fine prints are not often mentioned and it can be related to farmers' suicides and other things like that because trade produces winners and losers.

The Issue of Redistribution

Those who know a little bit of trade theory will recognize that I am talking about the Stolper-Samuelson theorem. So if we say that India is going to gain or a developing country is going to gain from international trade you are in some sense saying that there is a redistributive mechanism that is transferring some resources from the gainers to the

*Speech delivered by Partha Sen, Director, Delhi School of Economics, at the UGC Sponsored National Level Conference of Centre for Economic Studies, Presidency University, Kolkata on August 30, 2010.

losers. In India if there is so much disquiet over international trade, my presumption is that it is because the redistribution has not taken place, though it might be that losers are more entrenched politically. Clearly the issues of mining are the issues, where we are asking a bunch of tribal people who were marginalized even before India were integrated into the rest of the world to move out of their health and home because international trade has now made available for our market for minerals which was not there in the past. We have to look at 9.2% growth in that context and farmers' suicides[1] also in that context. There were redistribution possibilities but evidently that has not taken place.

If we believe that redistribution has taken place then everyone can become better off through trade. Now he is entitled to ask: if we are allowed to sell our goods abroad because it fetches us higher price why isn't he as a business allowed to borrow from the cheapest source abroad? If trade in goods is welfare improving (assuming a redistributive policy in place) why isn't trade in financial assets treated at par? If we are to differentiate between trade in goods and trade in assets, in case of the former, notionally, if I sell her apple and she sells oranges to me in exchange, the trade is over. In asset market borrowing and lending involves time, involves writing a contract, and involves someone honoring that contract. Again, not everything can be written down. Therefore, courts have to be there. So there has to be an overseeing mechanism. For want of a better word let us call that overseeing agency the State. So even in the abstract world of the neoclassical world you require a government to enforce financial trades. So if trade in financial assets is to be regulated you cannot have free trade in assets. Free trade in assets is a contradiction in terms. There must be some government agency to see to it that a mechanism is in place to enable the lenders to take actions that may be necessitated by moral hazard problems of imperfect information (I took a loan but I do not repay and I say that I put it in a factory but the factory did not produce output; I have sown this farm but there is no rain..)

Capital Flows: The Theoretical Underpinnings

Now I come to the issue of capital flows. In the early 1990s (1993-94 is more like it, not 1990-91) India opened up to international trade. We

[1] Farmers' suicide may have multiple causes like problems of insurance and lack of rationality on the part of the farmers.

removed a lot of our controls. We reduced our tariff rates; a lot of physical restrictions on trade were removed. We are a much more open economy today than we were in 1990-91 or than we have been historically (That's the danger that I want to come back to that India now trades a lot with the rest of the world). That is all right with the proviso I mentioned earlier that we need a strong State to redistribute the gains from trade, which was not what the Indian State were. Indian State was in the retreat in the early 1990s. But that is not the issue here. What Dr. Manmohan Singh did as the Finance Minister in the early 1990s was to open up capital account considerably. So we opened up the current account but we did not open up the capital account completely. There were restrictions on domestic firms' lending and borrowing abroad, but to inflows we were opened up almost completely. There were some restrictions on debt flows but that too have over time been brittled away.

What are the problems of an open capital account that has been faced by developing countries? Before I address that issue let me say one thing. If you look at the successful liberalizers, the countries which have integrated themselves with the rest of the world and traded and grown, these are the economies in the East Asia and South-East Asia. Japan was the first country, then we have slowly Taiwan, South Korea, Singapore, Thailand, Indonesia, Malaysia, and, of course the spectacular recent entry into this category: China. China has proved many of us wrong. Some 15/20years back while I visited China, I thought that China could not succeed by trading because it was so big , and that would cause disruptions in the world market. It did some disruptions, but it was successful in using international trade to work itself out of poverty. There are countries in Latin America which opened up their capital account as well as their current account. Experience of these countries is interesting—there is growth in these countries, but their growth is interspersed with collapses. If we look at Argentina it was probably the 7th or the 8th richest country in the world in the 1920s and look where it is now. It is in a way similar to India in that there are large public sector unions, youth congress and the like though it is not as big as India—Argentina is a sparsely populated country. So the overwhelming experience of globalization can be summed up, without going into the minutiae, in just two sentences: those who have kept a lid on their capital account and loosened their current account could use globalization successfully. Those who opened up capital account have not used globalization successfully. That is the evidence.

The Empirics

What are the arguments in response to empirical issues at the theoretical level? There are many problems with capital flows, but let me flag one or two, the important ones. First, capital inflows have a problem, and that is what we find all around us in India all the time. What capital inflows do is it appreciates real exchange rate. It is like property boom. Suppose everybody wants to buy a piece of land at Rajarhat. In the end there is excess demand and prices of property will go up in Rajarhat . So it will make it a very poor destination for manufacturing if everything is booming in Rajarhat. This in the economics literature is called the *Dutch disease.* In 1973-74 when the first oil price shock took place the presumption was that among the west European countries it is the Netherlands which would do the best that the oil price had shot through the roof, because it had the North Sea gas and North Sea oil. But after the event it was seen that the Netherlands were one of the worst performers, if not the worst performer. What happened is that since everybody thought that the Netherlands would do well, everybody tried to buy property, shares and things like that in the country. In the aggregate it pushed up the Dutch asset prices. Among other things, the exchange rate appreciated. In terms of traded goods, in terms of manufacturing output, the Dutch economy collapsed. This is what is known as the *Dutch disease.* Since we know what Dutch disease is we have to inoculate ourselves against the Dutch disease. But that has not happened. So inflows cause a problem, success causes a problem, potential success causes a problem. So if we keep the capital account closed then even if everyone in the world thinks India is going to boom they cannot buy Indian assets and so the appreciation will not take place.

Then there is a problem with outflows. What happens with outflows is that it tends to be very sudden, and it tends to discipline both the good boys and the bad boys. The best example is the Latin American crisis in 1998. Suddenly financial capital flows to Latin America dried up. Had they done anything wrong? The answer is no. They were booming, they were growing very quickly. There was no problem with Latin American debt. Capital flows to Latin America dried up because Russia had defaulted on its debt. Was Russia a big trading partner of Latin America? There was no trade between Latin America and Russia. So it cannot be that since Russia has defaulted the Latin American export market is disappearing. All that happened is that since Russia had defaulted, banks in New York wanted to rebalance their books and in rebalancing their books they were recalling their loans from Latin America. The Latin Americans referred to this as the *Sudden Stop*--The experience was so traumatizing! The reversals take place unrelated to the economy's fundamentals and because something has happened somewhere else. Economists often call this *sun-spot.* Then there are all kinds of problem with developing countries. The best example of this is the *Asian crisis* when banks had made a huge dollar loan to a taxi company in Jakarta. Once capital flows got reversed and the Indonesian rupiah devalued there was no hope in hell that this taxi company getting its income in Indonesian rupiah would be able to repay its dollar loan. So it defaulted. There are all sorts of problems, some of which are particular to developing countries and some of which are very general.

Capital Flows and Monetary Policy

I will focus more specifically on capital flows and monetary policy and we may find this may have some bearing on how the Reserve Bank of India is today trying to fight inflation. Let us go through whatever I have said before, that India was unlike most developing countries in that it had relatively well-developed financial markets, there was FDI of colonial variety. It was in mining and plantation. Then there came Mrs. Gandhi's regime. There was financial repression and we got into a mess in the 1970s. In 1969 banks were nationalized. We could argue that it was a very good thing but once the banks were nationalized problems began. Liberalization began in 1990s. There was privatization and trade and capital flows were liberalized. Here there are some facts we are familiar with: services are about 50% of our GDP, industry and agriculture are about 25% each of GDP, but agriculture still employs 60% of people. This is important because if macro policies are to be development-oriented then we have to do something in removing 60% of the workforce producing 25% of GDP into more productive uses. These people's productivity is very low. Macro policy (or any policy) has to think about removing people from agriculture to more productive uses. We know it must be done coherently (not the kind of staff we have seen in West Bengal recently) and macro policy has to play a role. It is important since India has no tradition in macroeconomics. When I say that I am bit of a lone voice in the wilderness it is because India has no role model. In my generation people saw Amartya Sen and Jagdish Bhagwati and so. Lot of people went into trade theory and the blind alley of social choice theory, but none came into macroeconomic theory because there was no role model. For an economy which has no role for macroeconomics, it is important that two landmark developments in India were due to macro crisis. Mrs Gandhi Senior's populism began with the BOP crisis in mid 1960s and liberalization, the reversal of that populist policy, was also the consequence of a second BOP crisis. So it is ironic that we do not care about macroeconomics but macroeconomics seems to care about us.

What is it that has been happening in monetary policy? After the capital account had opened up, initially capital came to India very gingerly, very slowly, but then there have been surges, though it is not huge in volume. With the surge of capital inflows, India tends to go the Dutch way. There is a lot of pressure on the currency to appreciate. The Reserve Bank of India tries to stave that off. What it does is that it sells to the foreigners assets and asks them to take Indian money. So it intervenes and buys foreign exchange. That of course prevents a nominal appreciation. It prevents appreciation of nominal exchange rate, but if the process continues forever it could still cause real appreciation. So 'e' (the nominal exchange rate) may remain constant but 'p' (price level) rises faster than in the rest of the world and you have a real appreciation. The RBI is aware of that and so it goes out into the market and sucks out excess liquidity by selling government bonds. So at the end of the day if we look at the balance sheet of the RBI, its liability in terms of money is more or less the same, but it is the asset side of the balance sheet that has changed—in the asset side there is now lots of foreign exchange but very little bonds. So what is the thinking in the RBI? In some sense the RBI has done all right under the constraint. But the Reserve Bank's policy is not transparent at all. I give you here a quote from Y.V. Reddy who is supposed to be one of the most successful central bank governors, "...unorthodox policies have assured the stability of the Indian financial system...rather than achieving ritualistic compliance with pre-set rules." In effect he is saying that he doesn't believe in any policy. People talk about inflation targeting, but RBI is nowhere near that. He is saying he is discretionary and he is proud to be discretionary. That is a big worry, because I don't think that people in the RBI has that sound knowledge of macroeconomics.

FDI and Portfolio

That capital flow has been liberalized in response to the macro crisis and BOP crisis I want to distinguish between FDI and portfolio flows. Both FDI and portfolio flows cause the *Dutch disease*. But FDI, presumably, is required—not all of FDI , not in retail—but some of FDI is required to upgrade our industry so that they can export . FDI can help by bringing in newer and better technology. Though it causes the Dutch disease at least we can identify what the gains are. In case of FII, except for a few brokers who get richer, the gains are very difficult to identify. One way FII flows are supposed to help the real economy is this: the FIIs come and invest in the stock market, the stock market booms, and now I can raise funds at a rate cheaper than what my capital goods cost. That is Tobin's q. So Tobin's q is the only way economic theory can be used to justify portfolio flows. We have to look at some Indian firms' behaviour since liberalization, those who have been receiving FII flows. I don't see the Tobin's q in the Indian data. May be I am not looking at it properly, maybe there are not enough data, but I looked at a panel and it is very mixed. Nevertheless, FIIs are investing in listed securities. Capital account is completely open for FII flows. Outward FDI has been relaxed—software, mining, gas and, even, automobiles. Outward equity flows were restricted initially but some liberalization has taken place. In Table 4.1 as we come closer to the recent period aggregate GDP growth may have collapsed a little bit, but rest of the indices (broad money, wholesale price index, and current account balance as percentage of GDP) were all correct except the fact that already last year for which the data are available, i.e., 2008-09, the deficit in the current account was 4.9% of the GDP. That is a huge number. This is also true in the time series data relating to fiscal and revenue deficits 'figure of India (Table 4.2). Now let us consider the problem of the *Dutch disease* a little more seriously. Let us look at Table 4.3, Figures 4.1 and 4.2 for NEER (normal effective exchange rate) and REER (real effective exchange rate) since 1993-94. There has been steady depreciation of the nominal exchange rate. Real exchange rate has been moving much less, if at all. Look at the current and the capital account and we see net capital flows are huge. There has been a huge hike in the last ten years (Initially it was much larger but it was still in absolute terms not very large). What I want you to notice is the *Dutch disease*. When the capital flows are high, current account balance goes into a deficit. Let's look at Table 4.3 and we see what the RBI is trying to do. The real effective exchange rate has not moved very much. This is a 36 currency index. The graph that I have shown has 6 currencies. So there is some difference. What we see is a secular rise in the foreign exchange acquisition of India. I want to make one thing very clear. Indians lead a very bleak life. Whenever there is something to rejoice, find a developing country market, they overreact. When India wins a 20-20 cricket all the country waves the tricolor.

Table 4.1: Major Macroeconomic Indicators (% changes)

Fiscal Year	*Aggregate GDP*	*Broad Money*	*Whole-sale Price Index*	*Current Account Bal (% of GDP)*
1990–91	5.6	15.1	10.3	–3.1
1991–92	1.3	19.3	13.7	–0.3
1992–93	5.1	14.8	10.1	–1.7
1993–94	5.9	18.4	8.4	–0.4
1994–95	7.3	22.4	12.5	–1.0
1995–96	7.3	13.6	8.1	–1.7
1996–97	7.8	16.2	4.6	–1.2
1997–98	4.8	18.0	4.4	–1.4
1998–99	6.6	19.4	5.9	–1.0
1999–00	6.4	13.9	3.3	–1.0
2000–01	5.2	16.2	7.0	–0.6
2001–02	5.6	14.2	3.6	0.7
2002–03	4.3	12.8	3.4	1.3
2003–04	8.5	15.2	5.4	2.3
2004–05	7.5	30.7	6.5	–0.4
2005–06	9.5	37.0	4.4	–1.2
2006–07	9.0	28.5	5.4	–1.1
2007–08	9.3	22.3	4.7	–1.5
2008–09	6.7	17.5	8.4	–4.1

Table 4.2: Some Fiscal Indicators

Year	*Gross Fiscal Deficit (C+S)*	*Revenue Deficit (C+S)*
Annual Average 1990–91 to1994–95	7.8	3.7
Annual Average 1995–96 to 1999–2000	7.8	4.7
2000–01	9.6	6.6
2001–02	10.0	7.0
2002–03	9.5	6.6
2003–04	8.5	5.8
2004–05	7.5	3.6
2005–06	6.2	2.8
2006–07	5.6	1.3
2007–08	5.2	0.9
2008–09	4.6	0.5

Table 4.3: Exchange Rates of the Indian Rupee

Fiscal Yr	*₹/US $*	*Nominal Effective Exch. Rate**	*Real Effective Exch. Rate**	*Foreign exchange Reserves (US $ bn)*
1993-94	31.4	100.0	100.0	19.3
1994-95	31.4	98.9	104.3	25.2
1995-96	33.5	91.5	98.2	21.7
1996-97	35.5	89.3	96.8	26.4
1997-98	37.2	92.0	100.8	29.4
1998-99	42.0	89.0	93.0	32.5
1999-00	43.3	91.0	96.0	38.0
2000-01	45.7	92.1	100.1	42.3
2001-02	45.7	91.6	100.7	54.1
2002-03	48.4	89.1	98.2	76.1
2003-04	45.6	87.1	99.6	113.0
2004-05	44.9	87.3	100.1	141.5
2005-06	44.3	89.9	102.4	151.6
2006-07	46.3	85.9	98.5	199.2
2007-08	40.3	93.9	104.8	309.7
2008-09	46.0	86.1	94.3	252.0

*36 Currency export based (base 1993–94=100)

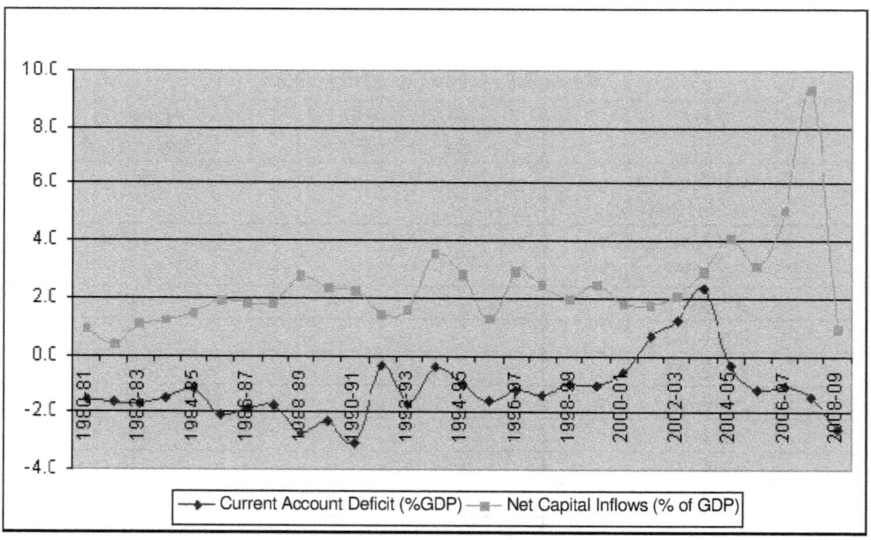

Fig. 4.1: Current and Capital Account Balances as % of GDP

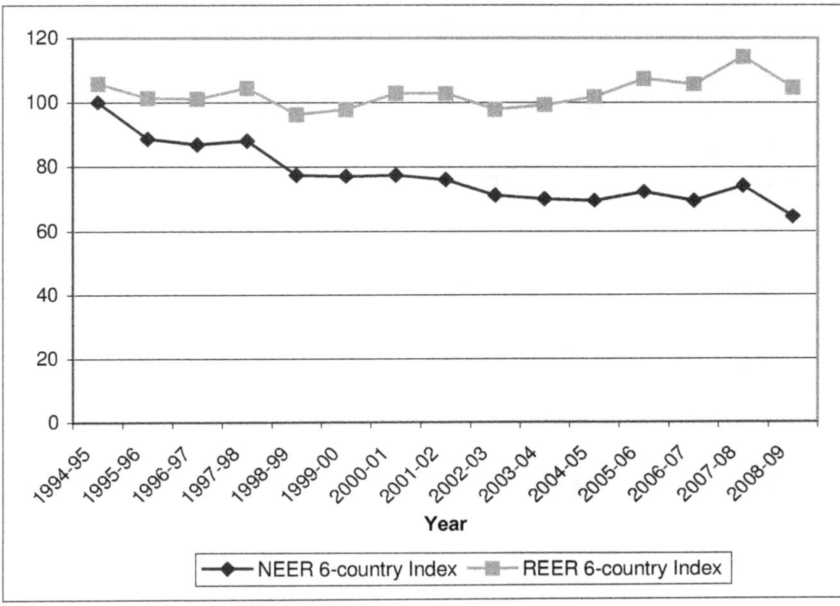

Fig. 4.2: Trends in Nominal and Real Effective Exchange Rate of Rupee

Foreign Exchange Reserve and the Infrastructure

In the aggregate data there was not much to cheer except the aggregate growth rate but since it was not coming to most of us we could not be pleased. But India is earning a lot of foreign exchange reserve. Therefore, aren't we a great national power? People who do not know macroeconomics are entitled to say this. I am very disappointed. You compare yourself with China. China is sitting on a mountain of foreign exchange, India is sitting on a very small hillock of foreign exchange. But can you measure the two in the same metric? The answer is no. China's foreign exchange reserves are its own. It has run current account surpluses. It has spent less than its foreign income and, therefore, it has acquired gold. India's foreign exchange reserve is all through its intervention in the foreign exchange market. So there is liabilities against these reserves, and if a reversal were to take place, our foreign exchange reserves will go out in one minute, since FII are fully repatriable. So you cannot use this stock of foreign exchange to build, say, infrastructure. Capital inflows were massive (miniscule compared to China, though), which peaked in 2007-08 (FDI \$34.2 b, Portfolio \$29.3b). There is tendency for the currency to appreciate. RBI intervenes in the foreign exchange market by buying foreign exchange. Money supply tends to go up as a result (Table 4.4). RBI runs out of government securities. The ultimate result is that foreign exchange reserves goes up, with lower RBI holding of government bonds. Though this prevents real appreciation of currency and limits *Dutch disease*, this gives rise to *quasi-fiscal cost.* Effectively, the RBI is exchanging low return foreign exchange holdings for high interest government bonds. This policy would become untenable as the RBI continues to accumulate foreign exchange reserves and thus driving up interest rates.

Table 4.4: Sources of Reserve Money Growth (Rs bn)

	RMC	*NFAC*	*NDAC*
Annual Average 1990–91 to 1994–95	183	137	46
Annual Average 1995–96 to 1999–2000	222	182	40
2000–01	227	313	–86
2001–02	347	668	–321
2002–03	309	942	–633
2003–04	675	1262	–588
2004–05	526	1284	–758
2005–06	839	602	237
2006–07	1359	1931	–572
2007–08	2194	3699	–1505

RMC: *Changes in reserve money*

NFAC: *Changes in net foreign exchange assets of RBI*

NDAC: *Changes in net domestic assets of RBI*

India has given up on manufacturing, because its capital account is so open. The trade balance is primarily what manufacturing and merchandise trade balance is. The deficit is 7 or 8% of GDP. There is no denying the fact that we are going the Latin American way and not the South-East Asian way. Trade balance is negative. The current account has also become negative. Initially trade deficit was financed by invisibles and transfers but the latter two have not grown to match the negative trade balance.

The Asset Market

Before I come to my last point let me say one thing which I should have said at the very outset. An underdeveloped asset market, a developing economy characteristic, is something which is subject to a lot of volatility. A good asset market is a deep asset market. A deep asset market is where there are players with different views of the future. Indian asset market, like most developing countries' asset markets, tends to be thin. How do we measure thinness? The only measure of thinness is that they are prone to excess volatility. On any given day it is either all buy-buy or all sell-sell. A good asset market is that which moves very little. What we see here are huge swings. It is mind-boggling. How thin the markets are! Most markets are moved by 40 or 50 thousand assets. Here asset markets are worth so many trillion dollars, but there are so few players!

Concluding Remarks

Liberalization has proved a lot of us wrong. Many of us believed that if we liberalize, the manufacturing would get wiped out. But that has not happened. Indian manufacturing has shown a lot of resilience. But the reality is not encouraging: although there have been too much capital flow, there appear too little infrastructure building and too little human capital formation. Fiscal deficit is too high, we have not been privatizing enough. Structural transformation is a non-starter. There is still 60% of population in agriculture. The external sector, the exchange rate, should be the very serious concern in any industrialisation strategy.

Industrialisation is not an unmixed blessing. There was such a lot of problem of land acquisition in West Bengal. I think it is a political problem. It is not a problem of industrialization per se. There was a credibility problem of a regime that closed down industry and suddenly wanted to industrialize overnight. It was a political credibility problem. Imagine we have to drag half a million population or even quarter of a million population out of poverty. What are the environmental cost and things like that? I am not minimizing the importance of these costs. But I am saying the only market-oriented way for such a huge economy like India to pull itself out of poverty has to be industrialization and there we have crippled industrialization by allowing too much of capital inflow.

Taxation, Income Distribution and Economic Growth in India: Principles, Theory and Empirics

Debnarayan Sarker*

Introduction

What should be the policy framework of taxation in Indian economy? It is well known that India has deliberately embarked on a programme of economic development and has gone it for economic planning for this purpose. But Indian planning is not merely intended for increasing the national income or accelerating the rate of economic growth. The objectives of the social and economic programmes have been formulated in specific terms in the Directive Principles of state policy embodied in the Constitution. The cardinal emphasis in this document is on the securing of "a social order, in which justice—social, economic and political—shall inform all the institutions of natural life" (cited in Rao, 2008:40). More specifically, the Directive Principles include the right of all men and women to an adequate means of livelihood, and "within the limits of its economic capacity and development, to make effective provision for securing the right to work, education and public assistance in the event of unemployment, old age, sickness and disablement or other cases of undeserved want" (*ibid*). In the economic sphere, this Directive Principles require the state "to direct its policy in a manner as to secure the distribution of ownership and control of the material resources of the community to sub-serve the common good and to ensure that the operation of economic system does not result in the concentration of wealth and the means of production to common detriment" (*ibid*). Economic development in India has, therefore, not only look to the requirements of growth but also to those of a social order based on social justice and the leveling down of inequalities. So, the taxation policy framework of India should be framed in such a way that the redistribution policy of public expenditure generating from tax income may incorporate the requirements of both—positive income growth from the standpoint of continuing the rise in income, savings, investment and entrepreneurial activities as the means of positive factor for the promotion of economic

---

*Revised version of the speech delivered at the UGC Sponsored National Level Conference of Centre of Economic Studies, Presidency University, Kolkata on August 28, 2010.

growth and the directive principles of constitution from the point of view of social justice together with the leveling down of inequalities.

Why is the redistribution of income for social justice and the leveling down of inequalities so important for policy framework of taxation in Indian economy? As is well-known, redistribution of income for the promotion of economic growth in a developing country like India is primarily intended to transfer income from spenders to savers, and from savings to investment. It is also intended to transfer income from non-producer to producers and to serve as an incentive to entrepreneurial activity. Obviously, a change in the pattern of income distribution with income diverted into the hands of those who will save or invest or undertake entrepreneurial activity, is a positive factor for the promotion of economic growth. So the redistribution of income merely for the promotion of economic growth is much favorable for the little section of people of Indian economy, who save, invest and undertake entrepreneurial activity. The practical experience is that despite all the well-intended plans and programmes and reasonably good growth since the early nineties in Indian economy, this rapid growth has failed to generate enough employment and livelihood opportunities for the poor. Poverty, one of the starkest manifestations of 'exclusiveness', has remained at unacceptably high levels and income inequality has also been grown up significantly.

So, the redistribution of income viewed from the standpoint of social justice and the leveling down of inequalities as laid down in the Directive Principles of constitution is mainly the response to the wishes of masses, who are the overwhelming majority of Indian people, because their key distribution issues are at stake. This paper, however, tries to examine the underlying factors influencing the principles of taxation policy of India and to look into its theoretical implications on reality for broader policy framework in Indian perspective. While examining the underlying factors influencing the principles of taxation policy of India, this paper tries to review the structure of Indian economy in terms of change in sectoral composition of GDP, occupational structure, per capita incomes and sectoral growth rate, economic structure of workforce, and the wider disparity between India's employment growth and GDP growth in relation to other growing Asian nations. They appear in Part II. Theoretical framework of taxation policy based on the review of the practical experience of Indian economy is contained in Part III. Part IV presents a short review of performance of such theoretical framework of taxation in Indian context. Part V concludes.

PART II

Economic development in India over a period of half a century seems to have made structural changes of the national economy with four basic issues: (a) swift transition of economy's share of GDP (in percentage) directly from an agricultural to service economy (b) the shift and change of sectoral work from agricultural to non-agricultural is much lower than the shift in sectoral share of GDP, (c) the ratio of per-worker agricultural to non-agricultural worker' income has been much wider and (d) the consumption expenditure for more than three-fourth of population has been severely at stake.

As regards the first issue is concerned, the share of agriculture in GDP has declined from about 55.4 per cent in 1950–51 to 18.5 per cent in 2006–07 (Table 5.1). That of industry has increased from about 16.1 per cent to 26.4 per cent in 2006–07. But the share of services has increased from about 28.5 per cent to about 59.5 per cent in 2006–07. The most striking feature of the structural change in the Indian economy in recent decades has been the pre-eminence of service sector as the major contributor to growth, rising its share rather sharply in the national output. Industry, particularly manufacturing, which has been observed historically to be the main contributor to growth, at least in the initial period of economic development, has played only a minor role in India's economic growth in recent years.

Table 5.1: Sectoral Share in GDP (in percentage) in India between 1950–51 and 2006–07 at 1993–94 prices

Sectors/Years	*50–51*	*60–61*	*70–71*	*80–81*	*90–91*	*00–01*	*06–07*
Agriculture and Allied	55.4	50.9	44.5	38.1	30.9	26.6	18.5
Industry	16.1	20.0	23.6	25.9	30.0	25.0	26.4
Services	28.5	29.1	31.9	36.0	39.1	48.4	59.5
Total	100.0	100.0	100.0	100.0	100.0	100.0	100.0

Source: Compiled from CMIE, Basic Statistics Relating to the Indian Economy, Vol. I, All India, August 1993 and Economic Survey, Government of India, Relevant issue, cited in Konar (2008:87).

Regarding the sectoral issue is concerned, the occupational structure of India clearly reflects the backwardness of the Indian economy (Table 5.2). Between 1951 and 2001, that is, within a period of 50 years the proportion of working population engaged in the primary sector consisting of agriculture and allied activities shows only a marginal decline from about 72 percent in 1951 to 60 per cent in 2001. In 2001, we see that in the tertiary sector about 4.8 per cent more worker have been employment with a period of 50 years (in 1951,about 17.2 per cent of total employed was contributed to service sector, whereas in 2001 it works out to about 22 per cent).However in the secondary sector the percentage of employment was about 10.7 percent in 1951, whereas in 2001 it was about 18 per cent ,the additional employment being about 7.3 percent over 50 years. The data on sectoral composition of rural workers [based on US (usual status)-PS (principal status) +SS (secondary status) concept] in 2004–05 also shows that rural workers are highly concentrated on primary sector. It reveals that out of total employed workers about 77.87 per cent are employed in rural areas in 2004–05 (Planning Commission, 2010:81). 72.56 percent of rural employed workers are employed in agricultural and allied activities and 13.87 percent are engaged in service sector. Since a large proportion of population is dependent on the primary sector it is a clear indication of the prevalence of the large scale disguised unemployment in agriculture and low per capita labour productivity and prevalence of large scale poverty.

Table 5.2: Occupational Classification of Workers (in percentage) in India Between 1951 and 2001

Sectors/Years	*1951*	*1961*	*1971*	*1981*	*1991*	*2001*
Primary Sector	72.1	71.8	72.1	68.8	66.8	60.0
Secondary Sector	10.7	12.2	11.2	13.5	12.7	18.0
Tertiary Sector	17.2	16.0	16.7	17.7	20.5	22.0
Total	100.0	100.0	100.0	100.0	100.0	100.0

Source: Statistical outline of India, 2002–03, page 14, Tata Services Limited, Department of Economics and Statistics and RBI, cited in Konar (2008:87).

Importantly, what distinguishes the Indian case from others in the group of some Asian countries most is the wider difference in the growth of employment vis-à-vis of GDP in services (Table 5.3). In all other countries (China, Philippines, Indonesia, Thailand, Malaysia, Republic of Korea, Pakistan) the share of services has increased more or less in line with that of GDP; in India, the employment share has shown much smaller increase than the GDP share. It implies that growth of services in India has been much less employment-intensive than other countries indicating that per worker agricultural to services income is much wider and discriminating for overwhelming majority of Indian people compared with other Asian countries.

Table 5.3: GDP and Employment shares in Services in some Developing Asian Countries (2002)

Country	*Share (per cent) in GDP*	*Share(per cent) in Employment*
China	34	31
Indonesia	38	39
Thailand	48	33
Philippines	53	47
Malaysia	44	50
Republic of Korea	55	62
Pakistan	54	34
India	51	22

Source: World Development Indicators 2004 (CD-ROM), World Bank, cited in Papola (2006:18, Table 3)

As regards the third issue is concerned, with about 50.9 per cent share in GDP and about 71.8 per cent share in employment, the ratio of per worker agricultural to non-agricultural incomes in 1960 was 1:3; in 2002 with 60 percent workers and about 21 percent GDP in agriculture, it is close to 1:6. Ratio between agriculture and service is 1:7, and between agriculture and industry, 1:4 (Papola, 2006:22-23).What it implies is that with sharp increase in the share of GDP in services, the gap between per worker agricultural to non agricultural income has substantially increased because the growth of GDP in services is accompanied by a much slower increase in the employment share of services. Also noteworthy is that the sectoral growth in recent years has made significant progress in non-agricultural sector. During the ninth plan period (1997–98 to 2001–02), GDP growth in India was 5.5 percent of which the growth of agriculture, industry and Services were 2.0, 4.6 and 8.1 per cent respectively, whereas during tenth plan period (2002–03 to 2006–07) GDP growth was accounted for 7.2 per cent of which the growth of agriculture, industry and services were 1.7, 8.3 and 9.0 per cent respectively (Planning Commission, 2006). So, employment structure is getting sharply polarized between a few high-end jobs in large corporations and the mass of low-productive low earning jobs in the unorganized sector. The service sector is particularly characterized by large differentials in earnings, with a few jobs in high tech activities with very high salaries and benefits, on the one hand, and a large mass of low-earning jobs in the informal sector, on the other. All these facts imply that significant majority of employed worker in India are employed in agriculture and allied activities and per worker wage rate of those workers is much lower than that of non-agricultural workers.

As to the fourth issue is concerned, it is important to be noted that not only does agriculture occupy the unorganized workforce of the country, but also has the non-agricultural workforce contributed the overwhelming majority under unorganized workforce. The National Commission for Enterprise in the Unorganized Sector (NCEUS) prepared estimates of employment in the unorganized sector. As on January 2005, the total employment (principal and subsidiary) in the Indian Economy was 458 million, of which the unorganized sector accounted for 395 million, that is, 86 percent of total workers in 2004-05.

On the basis of 2004–05 NSS data, NCEUS has also made an attempt to categorize the population of the country into six groups based on consumption. Extremely poor are those with a per capita per day (pcpd) consumption expenditure of the three fourths of the official poverty line (i.e., an average of Rs. 8.9 pcpd). They constitute 6.4 per cent of total population. The second group poor, who constitute 15.4 per cent of population, are those between extremely poor and up to the official poverty line (average expenditure of Rs. 11.6 pcpd). The third is called the marginally poor, who constitute 19 per cent of total population, with per capita consumption expenditure of only 1.25 times the poverty line (i.e. Rs. 14.6 pcpd).These three poor constitute 41 per cent of total population with a per capita consumption expenditure of Rs. 14.6 pcpd or below. The fourth called vulnerable (36.2 per cent of total population) have a per capita consumption expenditure of about two times of poverty line (i.e. Rs. 20.3 pcpd). However if the vulnerable are added to this group , the total accounts of 77 per cent of total population (Table 5.4) have a per capita consumption expenditure of Rs. 20.3 pcpd or below (or roughly below $ 2 ppp). These population belong to the households of the workforce employed in the unorganized sector or informal Indian economy. It is also observed that the absolute labour productivity in the organized sector is well above that of the unorganized sector in the economy as a whole. The labour productivity in the organized sector was about three times that in the unorganized sector in 1983, it grew to nearly 7 times in 2004-05 (National Accounts Statistics, CSO, and NSSO, various rounds, cited in Bandyopadhyay, 2009:31). This divergence of labour productivity is due to, other things remaining the same, the capital per worker ratio increases much more in the organized sector compared to the unorganized sector in both manufacturing and services (*ibid*). This divergence of labour productivity points to a substantial wage difference and wage inequality between skill categories of workers and unskilled ones reflecting that the benefits of economic growth of India has failed to trickle down to the bottom section of the labor market, i.e. the unskilled categories of workers.

Table 5.4: Consumption Expenditure (per capita per day) for Majority of Population in India (2004–05)

Category of Population	*Percentage of Population (%)*	*Expenditure (in Rs.) per Capita per Day (pcpd)*
Extremely poor	6.4	8.9
Poor	15.4	11.6
Marginally poor	19.0	14.6
Vulnerable groups	36.2	20.3

Source: NCEUS (2007) categorize the population of the country based on NSSO (2004-05)

PART III

Hence the vital issue is: What should be the framework of taxation in the structure of Indian economy where employment structure has been polarized between a few high-end jobs in large corporations and the mass of low-productive low earning jobs in the unorganized sector so that the redistribution of public expenditure can incorporate both the Directive Principles of constitution and the requirement of positive income growth? A particular policy instrument may be the imposition of tax on capital income (both physical and human capital) and the government spending on productive services which enhances labour income reflecting thereby to capture a much broader set of redistributive policies—redistributive policies may interact with growth enhancing policies.

Several papers (Bertola, 1993; Perotti, 1992; Fernandez and Rogerson, 1992; Barro, 1990; Alesina and Rodrik, 1994) have political models linking income distribution and growth. We try to establish theoretical framework in an economy where wage income is evenly distributed within overwhelming majority of Indian workers (about 86 per cent of total workers in India in 2004–05), whose labour productivity and per capita income level is much below compared with the minority, who possess high salaries and benefits along with high labour productivity. We assume that the imposition of tax on capital income including the human capital' income of skilled labour is the only source of government's income and the government spending is made on productive services through which this instrument enhances labour income to the owners of unskilled labour reflecting a common economy wide growth rate along a steady-state path which is independent of initial distribution of factor endowments, the distribution of factor ownership being time-invariant.

The theoretical framework uses a simple endogenous growth model with labour and capital as the primary factors of production. It takes the following assumptions:

1. Capital—an accumulated factor—is interpreted in the broad sense as including physical capital, human capital and all property technology.
2. Private production requires the provision of public services (which for concreteness we can think as "law and order services").
3. It is a simple endogenous growth which requires non-diminishing returns to the economy's reproducible resources.
4. Output is linear in capital and public services taken together.
5. A single good produced can be used for either C or I, and we fix its price at unity.
6. It rules out expropriation of capital. It leaves out consideration of expropriation, to avoid dealing with time-inconsistency problems in capital taxation, and it is not our focus.
7. Wage income is relatively evenly distributed. For Indian perspective, for example, they consider the laborers that work with low-productive and low earning jobs, who are the overwhelming majority of Indian workers and that of Indian population. So, wage income is considered here as income of unskilled labour force.
8. The unskilled labour force, which is taken to be constant (Labour is supplied inelastically, which allows us to set the economy's aggregate labour endowment (L) equal to unity), is not subject to taxation. It is built into the model to allow to discriminate between two types of factors of production-capital and labour, and to undertake distributive policies.
9. Income of labour force with relatively high productive and high earning jobs is considered as income for capital (human capital).
10. Linear tax is imposed on capital income.
11. Perfect competition is assumed in the factor market.
12. The agents have an infinite horizon which is taken as $\ln t \rightarrow \infty$.
13. Here taxes are used not only for redistributive purposes. Tax revenues provide a public good necessary for private production.

The aggregate production function is:

$$Y = VK^{\alpha}S^{1-\alpha}L^{1-\alpha}\ 0 < \alpha < 1, \qquad \ldots (1)$$

V is a technological parameter, K and L are the aggregate stocks of capital and labor, respectively, and S is the aggregate level of government spending on productive services. To save on notations, the time dependence of each variable is not shown here. The appeal of this model is that it attributes a constructive role for government. Therefore, redistributive policies will interact with growth-enhancing policies. Fiscal redistribution often takes place through various spending programs above and beyond direct cash transfers. To finance spending on public services, the government has access to a tax on capital income, γ. The budget is balanced every instant, so that

$$S = \gamma K \qquad \ldots(2)$$

[assume S is increasing linearly in K]

Despite the fact that this model rules out progressivity of tax as it allows only a linear tax on capital ,this model will effectively yield a form of progressive taxation with richer individuals (with higher capital income) being taxed more heavily than poorer ones—the median, because wage income is assumed to be relatively evenly distributed. Capital is to be interpreted here in broad sense namely as including physical capital, human capital and all proprietary technology. The tax on capital therefore should be viewed as a tax on all resources that are accumulated, including human capital.

Wages and rates of return on capital are determined by the usual marginal productivity conditions since we assume perfect competition in factor markets. As labour is supplied inelastically, which allows us to set the economy's aggregate labour endowment (L) equal to unity.

Taking appropriate partial derivatives of (1) and substituting from (2), we obtain,

$$r = \frac{dY}{dK} = \alpha V\gamma^{1-\alpha}, \text{ where } L = 1 \qquad \ldots(3)$$

$$w = \frac{dY}{dL} = (1-\alpha)V\gamma^{1-\alpha}K \qquad \ldots(4)$$

(because L = 1)

It is noted that the marginal productivity of capital is independent of the capital stock (K), once the tax on capital that finances government spending is taken into account. This prevents the operation of diminishing returns of capital.

Added to it, the MP_L and MP_K are both increasing in the tax rate on capital, since higher taxes allow more government spending on productive services for given level of K .

$$\left.\begin{array}{l}\text{i.e. if } \gamma \text{ increases } \dfrac{dY}{dL} \text{ increases} \\[2em] \text{if } \gamma \text{ increases } \dfrac{dY}{dK} \text{ increases}\end{array}\right\} \text{ for any given K}$$

If γ (tax rate) increases, wage income also increases because a higher rate of taxation allows the government increase its spending on services that increase labour productivity. The wage rate is also increasing in capital stock.

Also important is that as MP_K is independent of K, the higher rate of taxation will increase MP_K and also increase return on capital.

Then capital and labour income, net of taxes, are given by

$$Y^k = K(\alpha V \gamma^{1-\alpha} - \gamma) \qquad ...(5)$$

[Net of capital income = $(MP_K)(K)$ – cost of capital = $\alpha V\gamma^{1-\alpha}K - \gamma K$]

$$Y^L = (1-\alpha)V \gamma^{1-\alpha}K - \overline{C} \qquad ...(6)$$

[Net of labour income= $(MP_L)(L)$ – cost of labour = $(1-\alpha)\, V\, \gamma^{1-\alpha}KL - \overline{C}$

$= (1-\alpha)\, V\, \gamma^{1-\alpha}K - \overline{C}$ (as L = 1)]

For the national income identity to be satisfied, it is necessary that

$Y^k + Y^L + S = Y$, which is indeed the case here

$$[K(\alpha V \gamma^{1-\alpha} - \gamma) + \{(1-\alpha)V \gamma^{1-\alpha}K - \overline{C}\} + S] = Y.$$

However tax on capital plays two important role. First, for any given level of K, as tax rate on capital increases, marginal productivity of capital increases and so the return of capital(r) increases. But the tax on capital reduces net return to owners of capital, and hence may alter the incentive to accumulate. What it implies is that for a given level of K, as tax rate on capital increases return on capital increases which may induce the owners of capital for a positive incentive to accumulate capital, whereas from the standpoint of net return it may alter the incentive to accumulate. Second, Net wage income is increasing in tax because a higher rate of taxation allows the government increase its spending on services that increase productivity.

Hence the relevant issue is: if all individuals are assumed alike in all respects except the initial distribution of factor endowments (capital and labour) how does it affect on the common economy-wide growth rate, initial distribution of factor endowments and the rate of accumulation?

Each individual can earn income from both capital and labour. Therefore using (5) and (6) (i.e. net of taxes, capital and labour income for ith individual) we have

$$y^i = [\, K_i(\alpha V\, \gamma^{1-\alpha} - \gamma) + \{(1-\alpha)V\, \gamma^{1-\alpha}K - \overline{C}\,\}]$$

It appears that income of each individual depends on individual ownership of capital and on the aggregate stock of capital.

We assume that all individuals have the same logarithmic utility function. The consumption-saving decision of the ith individual is determined by solving the following problem:

$$\text{Max } U^t = \int_0^t \log N_i e^{-\rho t}\, dt$$

Such that $\dfrac{dK_t}{dt} = [\, K_i\,(\alpha V\, \gamma^{1-\alpha} - \gamma) + \{(1-\alpha)V\, \gamma^{1-\alpha}K - \overline{C}\,\} - N_i]$

$K(0) = K_0;\ K_t\,(\ln t \to \infty) = \text{free } (K_0, \text{given})$ ...(7)

Where N_i implies consumption of individual i and ρ is the discount rate.

The Hamiltonian function for the problem is as follows:

$$H(K,N,t,\lambda) = \log N_i\, e^{-\rho t}dt + \lambda[\, K_i(\alpha V\, \gamma^{1-\alpha} - \gamma) + \{(1-\alpha)V\, \gamma^{1-\alpha}K_i - \overline{C}\,\} - N_i] \quad ...(8)$$

Differentiating with respect to N_i (control variables) and setting equal to zero

we get $\dfrac{1}{N_i}e^{-\rho t} - \lambda = 0$

or, $\lambda = \dfrac{1}{N_i}e^{-\rho t}$ ...(9)

And the complementary costate condition is

$$\lambda = -\lambda\, \{\alpha V\gamma^{1-\alpha} - \gamma) + (1-\alpha)\, V\gamma^{1-\alpha}\} \quad ...(10)$$

The procedure now is to be eliminated the costate variable and defines a steady state solution. To this end, we differentiate (9) with respect to time

$$\lambda = -\rho\frac{1}{N_i}e^{-\rho t} \qquad ...(11)$$

We equate (11) with (10) and eliminate λ using (9) to define a steady-state equilibrium

$$\rho = (\alpha V\gamma^{1-\alpha} - \gamma) + (1-\alpha)\, V\gamma^{1-\alpha} \qquad ...(12)$$

Each individual then accumulates along a steady-state path as

$$\hat{K}_i = \hat{N}_i = (\alpha V\gamma^{1-\alpha} - \gamma) + (1-\alpha)\, V\gamma^{1-\alpha} - \rho \equiv \mu(\gamma) \qquad ...(13)$$

Here $\mu(\gamma)$ is the common economy-wide growth rate, which is independent of initial distribution of factor endowment. All individuals accumulate at the same rate. Also, the distribution of factor ownership is time-invariant.

For sufficient condition Arrow's theorem states that if maximum principle conditions are to be both necessary and sufficient, the maximized Hamiltonian must be concave in state variable (here k) for any given λ (The solutions appear in the appendix).

In our theoretical framework, we focus on capital taxation because this seems to be the simplest way of formalizing redistributive policy. But redistribution can be achieved by many other means: by progressive income and corporation tax, progressive indirect tax that hardly affects the expenditure pattern of the majority, by minimum wage laws, by imposing trade and capital restrictions, by the composition of government expenditure etc. The basic idea is that any government is likely to be responsive to the wishes of the majority when key distribution issues are at stake. The basic theoretical model discusses the links among factor ownership, redistributive policy and economic growth.

PART IV

Who bears the incidence of tax in Indian economy? Whatever the mode of tax system—direct or indirect—might be, if the incidence and shifting of tax burden hardly affects the poor, who are the overwhelming majority of Indian population, it does not seem to support the particular policy instrument (a tax on capital income) of our theoretical framework. During the second week of September 2010, food inflation rose to 15.46 per cent and overall inflation rate by about 8.5 per cent. Food inflation remained in double digits for seven consecutive weeks after touching a 13-month low of 9.53 per cent in the week ended July 24, 2010. Do these indicate that the incidence and shifting of tax burden hardly affects the poor, who are the overwhelming majority of Indian population? Certainly not. As regards the structure of taxation in India is concerned, almost all tax revenue state governments receive from their respective states are indirect tax revenue. Major tax revenue of state governments is sales tax which imposes high incidence on the consumption expenditure of the poor, who are the overwhelming majority of Indian population. However, concerning the tax structure of central government, one may find the trend of increase of direct taxation and a decline in indirect taxation in India during the period of economic reforms starting from 1990-91 onwards (Table 5.5). Increase in the rate of Direct tax in India usually implies higher incidence of capital tax, because the large mass of low-earning jobs in the informal sector are usually excluded from bearing the burden of tax; but the incidence of indirect tax has to be borne by them. It is true that taxation on commodities and services also contain an element of progression insofar as they fall on luxury consumption, but this is a comparatively small element. Impact of indirect taxation of India is an indication that the indirect tax has been at the cost of basic consumption of the masses. It seems to imply that the imposition of indirect tax system gives encouragement to those who have ability to consume and to save, and this must have proved favorable from the point of view of economic growth, though viewed from the point of social justice and the rising tax burden on the poorer classes, it makes tax burden to the large masses of low-earning jobs in the informal sector of Indian economy.

Table 5.5: Direct and Indirect Tax Revenue as percentage of Gross Tax Revenue (1990-91–2008-09)

Tax Revenue	*1990–01*	*1995–96*	*2004–05*	*2005–06*	*2006–07*	*2007–08*	*2008–09(RE)*
Direct	19.1	30.2	43.3	45.1	46.4	49.9	54.9
Indirect	78.4	69.1	56.1	54.4	51.0	47.0	44.8

Source: Budget Documents of the Central Governments. Government of India (2008, 2009).

Does government of Indian states spend her tax income on productive services? Is the redistribution of income almost used for the promotion of social justice and the leveling down of inequalities in Indian economy? Table 5.6 shows that social sector expenditure of Indian states which is usually used for the promotion of social justice and the leveling down of inequalities in Indian economy bears a minor part of state government' expenditure of Indian economy. The proportion of social sector expenditure ranges between 29.65 per cent and 38.56 per of total expenditure during the reform period. Development expenditure which includes expenditures on both social and economic overheads is around two third of total expenditure during reform period of Indian economy. Needless to say, a significant part of development expenditure is used for the financing of economic overheads which, in turn, increases the opportunities for investment, enterprise, and earnings in the private sector indicating that it is conducive to the promotion of economic growth.

Table 5.6: Development and Social Sector Expenditure as percentage of total Expenditure (1990-91–2008-09)

Expenditure	*1990–91*	*1995–96*	*2000–01*	*2004–05*	*2005–06*	*2006–07*	*2007–08*	*2008–09(RE)*
Development	69.6	64.6	60.5	51.8	58.8	59.7	61.7	65.2
Social Sector Expenditure	38.56	36.63	36.76	29.65	33.73	33.93	35.29	38.26

Source: Budget Documents of the State Governments, RBI (2010).

PART V

However the empirics of Indian economy seem to suggest that the poor, who are the overwhelming majority of Indian population and that work with low-productive and low earning jobs in the unorganized sector, are not free from taxation; rather the impact of indirect taxation of India is an indication that the indirect tax has been at the cost of basic consumption of the masses, the overwhelming majority of Indian population. Although it is a matter of positive sign that there is a declining trend of indirect taxation and increasing trend of direct taxation for the tax structure of central government in India during the period of economic reforms starting from 1990–91 onwards, the state governments' major tax income stem out from sales tax which impose high incidence on the consumption expenditure of the poor, who are the overwhelming majority of Indian population. Regarding redistribution issues are concerned, social sector expenditure of Indian states which is usually used for the promotion of social justice and the leveling down of inequalities in Indian economy, bears a minor part of state government' expenditure of Indian economy. It is also a great concern that about one third of the expenditure of government for Indian states during the current years is used for non-development purpose. All these facts, however, imply that, the taxation policy framework of India falls short to capture a much broader set of redistributive policies in keeping with the 'Directive Principles' of Indian constitution despite the fact that she has already achieved much higher rate of economic growth together with growing income inequality in the existing output and employment growth.

Although our theoretical framework focuses on capital taxation in order to explore the simplest way of formalizing taxable income, such a framework can be achieved by many other means: by progressive income and corporation tax, progressive indirect tax that hardly affects the expenditure pattern of the majority, by minimum wage laws, by imposing trade and capital restrictions, by the composition of government expenditure etc.. Added to it, government spending should be made on productive services so that workers of low earning jobs in the unorganized sector receive substantial benefit reflecting thereby to capture much broader set of redistributive policies which not only look to the requirements of growth but also to those of a social order based on social justice and the leveling down of inequalities in keeping with the 'Directive Principles' of Indian constitution.

References

Alesina. A and Rodrik. D (1994):"Distributive policies and Economic Growth", *The Quarterly Journal of Economics*, Vol. 109, No. 2, May, pp. 465–490.

Barro, R. (1990): "Government Spending in a Simple Model of Economic Growth," *Journal of Political Economy*, XCVIII, pp. 103–125.

Bertola, G. (1993): "Factor Shares, Saving Propensities, and Endogenous Growth," *American Economic Review*, LXXXIII, December, pp. 1184–98.

Bandyopadhyay, D.K. (2009): 'Wage-employment Determination in Indian Labour market under Economic Reform', *Artha Beekshan*, Vol. 18, No. 1, June, pp. 20–33.

Fernandez, R. and Richard R. (1992): "Human Capital Accumulation and Income Distribution," *NBER Working Paper* No. 3994.

Government of India (2008), '*Economic Survey, 2007–08*', Oxford University Press.

Government of India (2009), '*Economic Survey, 2008–09*', Oxford University Press.

Konar, D. (2008): 'Service-led Growth in India and Rural Poverty', *Artha Beekshan*, Vol.15, No. 3, December, pp. 85–97.

NCEUS (2007): 'Report on Conditions of Work and Promotions of Livelihoods in the Unorganized Sector', *Government of India*, New Delhi.

Planning Commission (2006): 'Approach to the Eleventh Plan', *Government of India,* New Delhi.

Planning Commission (2010): 'West Bengal Development Report', *Government of India ,* New Delhi.

Perotti, R. (1992): "Income Distribution, Politics, and Growth," *American Economic Review Papers and Proceedings*, LXXXII, May 1992, pp. 311–16.

Papola, T.S. (2006): 'Emerging Structure of Indian Economy: Implications of growing Intersectoral Imbalances', *The Indian Economic Journal*, Vol. 54, No. 1, April-June, pp. 5–25.

Rao, V.K.R.V. (2008): 'Redistribution of Income of Economic Growth in Under-developed Countries', *Indian Economic Journal*, Vol. 56, No. 2, July-Sep, pp. 34–56.

Reserve Bank of India (2010): State Finances: A Study of Budgets of 2009-10, *http://www.rbi.org.in/scripts/AnnualPublications.aspx?head=State%20Finances%20:%20A%20Study%20of%20Budgets.*

Saint-Paul, Gilles, and Thierry Verdier, "Education, Democracy and Growth," *CEPR Discussion Paper* No. 613, February 1992.

Appendix

The Hamiltonian function for the problem is as follows:

$$H(K,C,t,\lambda) = \log N_i\, e^{-\rho t}dt + \lambda[K_i(\alpha V\, \gamma^{1-\alpha} - \gamma) + \{(1-\alpha)V\, \gamma^{1-\alpha}K - \overline{C}\} - N_i] \qquad \ldots(8)$$

Differentiating with respect to c_i (control variables) and setting equal to zero

we get $\frac{1}{N_i} e^{-\rho t} - \lambda = 0$

or, $\overline{N}_i = \frac{1}{\lambda} e^{-\rho t}$....

Here $\overline{N}_i$ is independent of K_i. This allows N to be eliminated from the maximized Hamiltonian:

$$H(k, \lambda, t) = e^{-\rho t} + \lambda[K_i(\alpha V\, \gamma^{1-\alpha} - \gamma) + \{(1-\alpha)V\, \gamma^{1-\alpha}K - \overline{C}\}]$$

It is now a matter of showing that this function is concave in K. This is achieved by checking that the second order derivative of the maximized Hamiltonian with respect to K is non-positive.

$$\frac{dH}{dK} = \lambda[\, \alpha V\, \gamma^{1-\alpha} - \gamma) + \{(1-\alpha)V\, \gamma^{1-\alpha}\}]$$

$$\frac{d^2H}{dk^2} = 0.$$

As $\lambda \geq 0$; that is, the shadow price of K is non-negative, the condition of concavity is satisfied and a solution which satisfies the maximum principle necessary conditions is both necessary and sufficient.

Consumerism in India: A Study based on NSS Data

Rajnarayan Gupta

1. Introduction

Consumerism has two meanings in usage. Sometimes it means indulgence in consumption. Sometimes it is also used in the sense of protection of the consumer right or consumer sovereignty. In this study, however, consumerism has been defined in the first sense of the term; it refers to the spirit of consumption – the tendency to consume.

It is often said that consumerism is increasing in the world. Perhaps this conjecture appears sensible with the increasing commercialization of the society and with the ever increasing magnitude of advertisement for consumer goods and their constant pampering in the media, especially in the electronic media. The present study attempts to estimate the level of consumerism in India. It is a cross-section analysis and focuses on regional variations in the consumption pattern. The study contains four sections. Section 2 addresses the problem of measuring consumerism and provides some acceptable indices for that. Section 3 analyzes levels of consumerism in different states in India. The analysis is based on NSS (National Sample Survey) data. The study is concluded in section 4.

2. Consumerism—The Measurement Problem

Consumerism (the consumption spree), have nothing to do with essential commodities like food items or health services. The demands for those items are at inelastic. Even if people are motivated to speed up consumption, they are least likely to raise the consumption of essentials. Consumerism should affect the consumption of non-essential items or, more specifically, the luxury items. It is, however, very difficult to draw a dividing line between essential and non-essential commodities. The very concepts of 'essential' and 'non-essential' are relative. What was non-essential in the past has become essential in the present. Similarly, what is being considered as non-essential today may be regarded as essential in the future. Telephone and especially mobile phone was regarded as a luxury item when it was launched in the market. But now it has been an essential item, at least to a large section of the society. It is also very difficult to dub an item essential or non-essential uniformly for all classes of people. What is used as an essential commodity to the rich may appear quite luxurious to the poorest section of the society. A car or a computer set may be treated as an essential item by a rich or an upper middle-class family, but they are certainly luxuries to the poor.

However, in spite of all those difficulties, it would probably not be unwise to make some gross classification of consumer goods between essentials and non-essentials. Food items and health facilities, it has been mentioned above, can be regarded as essential commodities. Consumer durables, on the other hand, should grossly fall in the category of non-essentials. People can live without a television or a car, but they cannot live without food. One's consumption of food should not show much fluctuation. One cannot curtail it to a large extent even in bad times. Similarly, one does not increase it even in times of prosperity or even if one is guided by what may be called the spirit of consumerism. Consumption of consumer durables, on the other hand, seems to be vulnerable to consumerism among other things. Regarding other groups of consumption items, it is very difficult, however, to mark them essentials or non-essentials. Education, for instance, is almost a necessity to the middle-class salaried people, but it is certainly a luxury to the rich who have already accumulated considerable wealth. Education brings them social prestige and status. Education also seems to be luxury to the poor in view of the fact that most part of their income comes from blue collar occupations which do not require much education. Similar ambiguity remains in case of clothing. Clothing is necessary to the poor. They spend on clothing mainly out of necessity. But clothing appears to be a luxury to the rich or even to the middle-class. The major part of their expenditure on dresses is made for fashion purposes.

The present study concentrates on the consumption of durable goods. Since consumer durables are almost purely non-essentials to all classes of people, the level of consumption of those goods and their share in the consumer's budget can be treated as two indices of consumerism – the spirit of consumption. The study examines levels of consumerism in different states in India on the basis of data published by NSSO (National Sample Survey Organization).

NSSO conducts detailed survey of consumer expenditure throughout the country in every fifth year. NSS divides the population into several expenditure classes. Expenditure classes are typically called Monthly Per

Capita Consumer Expenditure (MPCE) classes. Total monthly consumer expenditure of a household is divided by the number of family members to get MPCE of that household. Data are provided on average monthly per capita expenditure on different broad groups of food and non-food items for different expenditure classes.

A household is defined to be a group of persons who live together and take food from a common kitchen. Temporary visitors are excluded from the household but temporary stay-aways are included. Household consumer expenditure is then the total expenditure of the household on various groups of items, viz., food, clothing, health, education, durable goods and others. The present study considers only the expenditure on consumer durables. By consumer durables the survey means all consumption items which have a lifetime of one year or more. Thus, durable goods include furniture, television sets, tape recorders, jewellery and ornaments, home appliances like washing machines or refrigerators and so on. Consumption expenditure on durable goods includes both expenditure on purchase and expenditure on repair and construction of household durables.

NSS collects data on expenditure with reference period of 30 days and/or 365 days. However, up to the 50th round survey, data were published only with the reference period of 30 days. The 55th round survey published data with both 30-day reference period and 365-day reference period. Data on five categories of goods and services, viz., clothing, footwear, education, medical services and durable goods were published with 365-day reference period, while data on all other types of goods and services were published with reference period of 30 days. The 61st round survey published data on all items with reference period of 30 days, but in addition, it also presented data on those five special categories of goods and services with 365-day reference period. The present study analyzes the report of the 61st round survey, the latest as yet.

3. Consumerism in Different States and Union Territories

The present study estimates consumerism in all states and union territories in India. Consumerism is measured by MPCE on Durable Goods (MPCEDG) and Budget Share of Durable Goods (BSDG). Data on MPCE and MPCEDG are available in the NSS report (61st round). Budget shares (BSDG) are then calculated from those two variables. However, NSSO conducts surveys separately for the rural sector and the urban sector and publishes data accordingly. Analysis of Consumerism has therefore been sector specific.

Table 6.1 presents MPCEDG and BSDG in all states and union territories in India. A wide variation in consumerism is observed in the data. Kerala shows the highest level of consumerism with average expenditure on durables of □ 97.08/- in the rural sector. It is followed by Himachal Pradesh (□ 50.14/-), Andaman & Niccober Islands (□ 42.89/-), Pondichery (□ 39.72/-), Daman & Diu (□ 38.6/-), Jammu & Kashmir (□ 38.44/-) and Haryana (□ 38.26/-). The states and union territories showing low consumerism, on the other hand, are Sikkim, Tripura, Jharkhand, Chandigarh and Bihar with average expenditure on durables of □ 4.72/-, □ 6.56/-, □ 8.58/-, □ 8.82/-, □ 11.47/- respectively, Sikkim occupying the lowest rank. In terms of budget share too, Kerala stands first in consumption of durables in the rural sector. Keralians spend 9.42 per cent of their budgets on durables. Kerala is followed by Pondichery, Chattisgarh, Jammu and Kashmir and Haryana with budget share of 5.11%, 4.85%, 4.77% and 4.23% respectively. Sikkim, at the other end, shows the lowest level of consumerism even in terms of budget share. Sikkimeese spend only 0.64 per cent of their budgets on durable goods. Among others exhibiting low budget shares of consumer durables are Chandigarh (0.95%), Tripura (1.28%), Jharkhand (1.95%) and Meghalaya (2.02%).

The picture in the urban sector replicates the rural scenario. Kerala, as in the rural sector, is the highest consumer of durable goods in terms of both MPCE on consumer durables and budget share and Sikkim the lowest. Keralians spend on average □ 143.29/- (monthly) on consumer durables which is 10.58 per cent of their average monthly per capita expenditure. Sikkimeese, at the other extreme, spend only □ 7.3/- on durables which occupy a mere 0.63 per cent of their average monthly (per capita) budget. In terms of MPCEDG, other states and union territories showing high consumerism are Andaman & Niccobar Islands (□ 118.23/-), Dadra & Nagar Haveli (□ 106.04/-), Lakshadweep (□ 83.42/-) and Goa (□ 77.69/-). The lowest figures, after Sikkim, are for Tripura (□ 1.48/-), Manipur (□ 1.55/-), Jharkhand (□ 1.69/-) and Meghalaya (□ 1.95/-). The rankings remain almost the same in respect of BSDG.

Table 6.1: MPCE, MPCEDG & BSDG

State/Union Territory	*Rural Sector*			*Urban Sector*		
	MPCE	*MPCEDG*	*BSDG*	*MPCE*	*MPCEDG*	*BSDG*
Andhra Pradesh	585.55	13.48	2.23	1018.55	35.98	3.29
Arunachal Pradesh	771.53	24.67	3.3	881.10	24.67	2.68
Assam	543.18	13.56	2.35	1057.99	35.42	3.13
Bihar	417.11	11.47	2.58	696.27	15.45	2.12
Chhatisgarh	425.10	21.6	4.85	989.97	61.83	6.42
Delhi	918.50	51.8	4.9	1319.31	34.35	2.42
Goa	985.49	36.68	3.59	1431.97	77.69	5.95
Gujarat	596.09	24.67	3.82	1115.20	70.16	5.82
Haryana	862.89	38.26	4.23	1142.35	49.63	4.19
Himachal Pradesh	798.11	50.14	6	1390.07	73.41	5.16
Jammu & Kashmir	793.16	38.44	4.77	1070.12	62.29	5.58
Jharkand	425.30	8.58	1.95	985.43	17.24	1.69
Karnatak	508.46	18.17	3.35	1033.21	31.64	2.78
Kerala	1013.15	97.08	9.42	1290.89	143.29	10.58
Madhya Pradesh	439.06	17.69	3.84	903.68	51.83	5.8
Maharashtra	567.76	20.74	3.48	1148.27	57.99	4.72
Manipur	614.20	15.96	2.46	726.38	11.8	1.55
Meghalaya	655.30	13.8	2.02	1190.09	24.57	1.96
Mizoram	778.35	18.42	2.19	1200.51	29.24	2.31
Nagaland	1010.81	35.58	3.39	1498.47	63.01	3.97
Orissa	398.89	16.45	3.9	757.31	28.9	3.66
Punjab	846.75	31.35	3.46	1326.09	58.4	4.47
Rajasthan	590.83	16.88	2.82	964.02	32.28	3.42
Sikkim	688.53	4.72	0.64	1106.79	7.3	0.63
Tamil Nadu	602.17	17.82	2.96	1079.65	45.04	3.86
Tripura	487.63	6.56	1.28	1000.54	14.79	1.48
Uttar Pradesh	532.63	21.98	4.07	857.05	32.62	3.72
Uttaranchal	647.15	20.7	3.19	978.26	52.59	5.18
West Bengal	562.11	20.69	3.59	1123.61	48.23	4.16
Andaman & Niccobar Islands	1069.08	42.89	4.03	1802.39	118.23	6.50
Chandigarh	862.75	8.82	0.95	1769.52	72.67	3.78
Dadra & Nagar Haveli	569.80	23.34	4.07	1407.50	106.04	7.17
Daman & Diu	1160.89	38.6	3.26	1079.59	36.74	3.38
Lakshadweep	1312.55	37.28	3.26	1421.22	83.42	6.43
Pondichery	735.31	39.72	5.11	1022.53	32.32	2.95

Table 6.2 gives the summary statistics. Remarkable disparity in consumption of durable goods across states and union territories is evident from the statistics. Disparity is observed in both the rural sector and the urban sector. Figs. 6.1 and 6.2 depict variations in consumerism in the 15 major states in the country. Variation is noticeably large. Kerala, in particular, deserves special attention as consumerism is incomparably high there. States like Bihar, Assam and others show, on the other hand, very low consumerism.

Table 6.2: Summary Statistics

	Rural Sector			*Urban Sector*		
	MPCE	*MPCEDG*	*BSDG*	*MPCE*	*MPCEDG*	*BSDG*
Mean	707.89	26.24	3.46	1136.74	49.74	4.08
Median	647.15	20.74	3.39	1079.65	45.04	3.78
Standard Deviation	229.21	17.45	1.56	257.73	30.45	2.01
Range	(1312.55, 398.89)	(97.08, 4.72)	(9.42, 0.64)	(1802.39, 696.27)	(143.29, 7.30)	(10.58, 0.63)

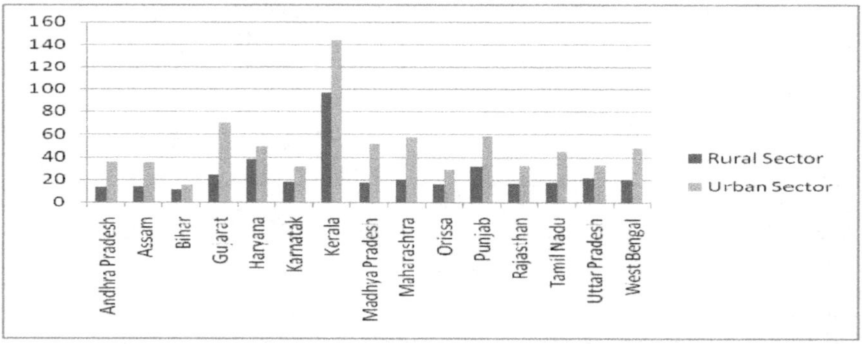

Fig. 6.1: Monthly Per Capita Expenditure (Rs.) on Durable Goods (MPCEDG)

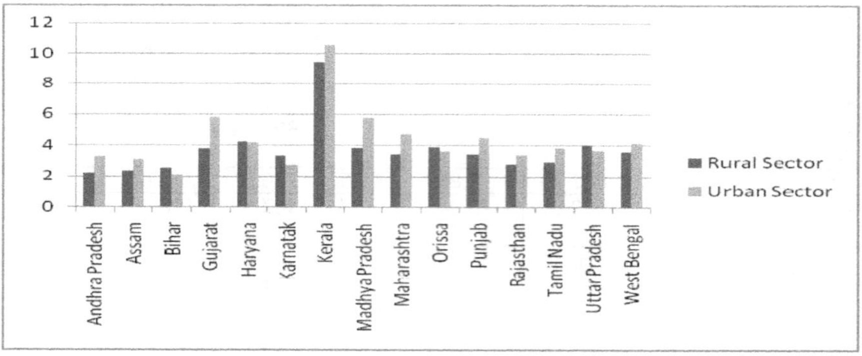

Fig. 6.2: Budget Share (%) of Durable Goods (BSDG)

However, disparity in consumerism is evident across sectors too. Consumerism is noticeably higher in the urban sector than the rural sector. Both MPCE on durables and budget share are higher in the urban sector than the rural sector for almost all states and union territories. The mean MPCEDG of the urban sector, for instance, is ₹ 49.74/- while that of the rural sector is ₹ 26.24/-. Similarly, the mean budget share is 4.08%

in the urban sector and 3.46% in the rural sector. Thus, the role of urbanization in inducing consumerism can not be ignored.

The variation in consumerism may be explained by variations in economic conditions of the people. Durable goods consumption seems to be higher among the rich people than the poor. It is the rich who can indulge in luxuries. The poor, on the other hand, spend relatively more on necessities. Therefore, MPCE on durable goods (MPCEDG) for a state or union territory should depend on its overall affluence. If MPCE[1] is taken to be a measure of the affluence of the state/union territory, then states/union territories with high MPCE should show high values of both MPCEDG and BSDG. The strong and positive correlations between MPCE and MPCEDG and between MPCE and BSDG are evident from the correlation matrices (Table 6.3 and Table 6.4). Particularly, the correlation coefficient is considerably high between MPCE and MPCEDG in both the rural sector (0.63) and the urban sector (0.68). Likewise, the sectoral variation in consumerism may also be attributed to variation in MPCE. In all states and territories, MPCE is considerably higher in the urban sector than the rural sector (Table 6.1). The mean MPCE, for instance, in the urban sector is □ 1136.74/- while that in the rural sector is □ 707.89/- (Table 6.2). Thus, overall, urban people are more affluent than rural people and perhaps that is the reason why they spend more on luxuries than their rural counterparts both in absolute and relative terms.

Table 6.3: Correlation Matrix Rural Sector

	MPCE	*MPCEDG*	*BSDG*
MPCE	1.00	0.63	0.25
MPCEDG	0.63	1.00	0.88
BSDG	0.25	0.88	1.00

Table 6.4: Correlation Matrix Urban Sector

	MPCE	*MPCEDG*	*BSDG*
MPCE	1.00	0.68	0.41
MPCEDG	0.68	1.00	0.92
BSDG	0.41	0.92	1.00

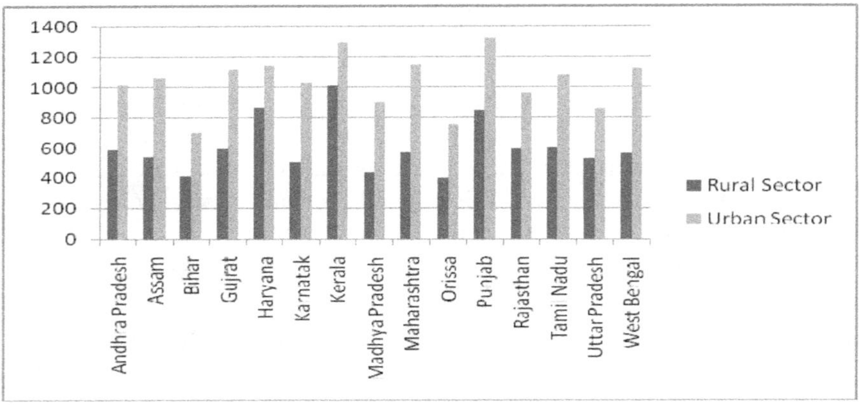

Fig. 6.3: Monthly Per Capita Expenditure (MPCE)

4. Conclusion

The present study attempts to measure consumerism in terms of spending on consumer durables. Consumer durables are mostly luxury goods. The same is, however, not true of other categories of consumer goods and services. The study is based on NSS data. The Report of the 61st round survey of the NSSO is considered for the purpose. The study finds wide disparity in spending on consumer durables across states and across sectors in India. Disparity is observed in absolute expenditure as well as in the budget share of durables. The variation in consumerism seems to be largely due to variations in the economic conditions of the people. Consumerism appears to be a reflection of income inequality in the country.

Note

1 Per capita state domestic product is a better measure of the economic condition of a state. However, data on it are not available with the rural-urban break up. Expenditure level, i.e., MPCE, is therefore considered as the proxy for income.

References

Krishnamurthy, S (2004), "Consumer Durables: Less pricey, more competitive", *The Hindu Business Line*, Jan 09.

NSSO (1989), *Level and Pattern of Consumer Expenditure,1987-88*, NSS 43rd Round, Ministry of Statistics and Programme Implementation, Government of India, New Delhi.

NSSO (1995), *Level and Pattern of Consumer Expenditure,1993-94*, NSS 50th Round, Ministry of Statistics and Programme Implementation, Government of India, New Delhi.

NSSO (2001), *Level and Pattern of Consumer Expenditure, 1999-00*, NSS 55th Round, Ministry of Statistics and Programme Implementation, Government of India, New Delhi.

NSSO (2006), *Level and Pattern of Consumer Expenditure, 2004-05*, NSS 61st Round, Ministry of Statistics and Programme Implementation, Government of India, New Delhi.

NSSO (1995), *Consumption of Some Important Commodities in India, 1993-94*, NSS 50th Round, Ministry of Statistics and Programme Implementation, Government of India, New Delhi.

NSSO (2001), *Household Consumer Expenditure in India: Key Results, 1999-2000*, NSS 55th Round, Ministry of Statistics and Programme Implementation, Government of India, New Delhi.

RBI (2007), *Handbook of Statistics on Indian Economy*, www.rbi.org.in.

Singh Sethi, Amarjit (2001), "Globalization and the Emerging Pattern of PFCE – The Indian Experience", *The Journal of Income and Wealth*, Vol. 23, No. 2, pp. 145-160.

Commercial Piracy: Cry for Crackdown and the Issue of Social Surplus

Debabrata Lahiri*

Motivation

The issue of commercial piracy is particularly relevant in developing countries with a large number of low end users (and a large section of them do not have easy internet access) of digital products like DVD music and movies as well as software with large network effect. Commercial piracy unlike end user piracy (peer-to-peer copying or unlawful downloading) does not have the effect of creating the potential for future demand for the legal version of the product. If it has any effect on the legal version of the product it is one of loss of demand. No wonder there is intense lobbying by the industry for harsh crackdown on piracy. Interestingly, the concern is not uniform for all industries. One question that arises is: Aren't all the digital industries equally affected by piracy?

This paper will try to approach this question by trying to conceptualize the existence or absence of piracy as a sub-game-perfect Nash equilibrium. There are three parties involved: the legal producer, the buyers, and the pirates. Since the interests of buyers and legal producers are antagonistic, any demand from any party for a change in the equilibrium solution must be judged in terms of the resultant change in social surplus. Any attempt to impose penalty on piracy by the Copyright Authority raises the value of the cost parameter for the pirate and establishes a new equilibrium in the market. It needs to be seen if this new equilibrium is acceptable from the standpoint of social surplus.

Literature Survey

The theoretical literature on digital piracy addresses two issues: the optimal strategy of the incumbent producers regarding the decision on copyright protection investment (entry deterrence), and the optimum policy of the copyright authority with respect to its decision on monitoring. Since there are both end-user piracy and commercial piracy

---

*The author is thankful to Malabika Roy, Department of Economics, Jadavpur University, for her comments on an earlier draft of the paper.

there are in effect four possible combinations to be examined, not always in isolation. While there is a fairly large literature on the incumbents' strategy to negotiate piracy (Joshua Slive and Dan Bernhardt, 1998; Oz Shy and Jacques-Fran̜çlois Thisse, 1999; Poddar, S., 2005 *et al.*), the theoretical literature on optimal policy of copyright monitoring in the presence of commercial piracy is relatively small. This is perhaps because the incidence of for-profit piracy is pronounced only in the developing countries and is not as pronounced a feature as end-user piracy in the developed nations. There is no doubt that the world over end-user piracy, particularly the internet piracy, engages by far the largest attention of the software as well as the entertainment industry. However, the issue of commercial piracy is also serious enough to merit a larger literature on the monitoring aspect than what exists at present. The existing literature gives the verdict in favour of not monitoring (Banerjee, D.S., 2006; Banerjee, D.S., Banerjee, T. and Raychoudhuri, 2008) though the legal producers will always try to prevent piracy (Poddar, S, 2005).

The rationale behind the above conclusion is that the grey market of digital copies has the potential to win away a part of potential buyers of original copies by offering them a throw away price in addition to creating a new market for itself. This raises the consumer surplus on one hand and reduces the monopoly profit of the legal sellers who can compete only by reducing price.

Methodology

This paper uses two equilibrium concepts. It first solves for the equilibrium in a monopoly setup. The paper then follows a dominant firm model of price leadership with the copyright producer as the dominant firm and commercial pirates as the competitive fringe. The format followed is that of a sequential game with complete and perfect information. At the initial node the copyright producer makes up her mind on the issue of development and marketing of a product with high development cost but insignificant marginal cost (MC). In the second stage she sets a price for the product in case she decides to market the product. At the third stage the pirates with insignificant fixed and marginal cost decide whether to enter or not to enter the market to sell a somewhat inferior quality of the product relative to the original. In case of entry the price charged by a typical pirate will be the MC of production, since in absence of any mentionable fixed cost they may be assumed to engage in a Bertrand competition.

The subgame-perfect Nash equilibrium of this game is analyzed and compared with monopoly equilibrium to explore the following:

(i) The condition under which the product will be developed and the market will exist under threat of unhindered piracy.

(ii) If the market exists under free entry of pirates, does piracy results in increased social surplus?

If the copyright producer finds it remunerative to develop and market the product even when the pirates freely operate in the grey market, and if the social surplus is higher than what is obtained under monopoly, it does not make any sense on the ground of social welfare to clamp down on the pirates to ensure monopoly for the copyright producer. However, a non-monopoly subgame-perfect Nash equilibrium involving no piracy under non-insignificant marginal cost of piracy will also be considered to see if an even better result is possible. The touchstone of judgment in this paper will be social surplus rather than the consumer surplus, because in a general equilibrium framework super-normal profit in a market is a source of consumption in other markets even though some of these markets may exist only in future to the extent supernormal profit is saved for investment. Further, primacy is placed on the copyright producer's production, because in absence of such production the derivative grey market does not see the light of the day and, therefore, the entire social surplus that this product could have contributed would be lost to the society.

The Model

Let us consider a product X which can be developed only at a large fixed cost – launching of a music CD or a movie DVD, or a bestseller like a Harry Potter novel involves considerable fixed cost including buying the selling right, hiring the services of technicians of different types, marketing expenses, share of fixed overhead cost and the like, in addition to normal profit. Marginal cost of such a product is typically too low to be considered significant, i.e., $MC \cong 0$.[1] In absence of large scale possession of copying machines by the consumers at large, the ones who own them have the potential to make quick money through commercial piracy.

Preferences of n potential consumers are assumed to be vertically differentiated. We are, therefore, restricted to the cases where consumers

[1] This is inclusive of normal profit, since in a typical developing country the opportunity cost of supplying enterprise is also close to zero.

do not differ on their appreciation of quality of the product. They differ only in their purchasing power – in their marginal rates of substitution (MRS) of other commodities (measured in money) for quality. Net utility or consumer surplus derived from consumption of one unit of X may be given by:

$$U = \theta s - p; \text{ where } \theta = \left.\frac{dp}{ds}\right|_{\bar{u}} \in (0, \bar{\theta}], \text{ where } \bar{\theta} \in R^{+} \tag{1}$$

s: quality index per unit of X ≥ 0 with higher value of s signifying better quality, p: price of X of quality s.

θ is assumed to be distributed uniformly over the interval $(0, \bar{\theta}]$ among the n prospective consumers.

Let $F(\theta)$ be defined as the proportion of consumers with values of MRS, $\left.\frac{dp}{ds}\right|_{\bar{u}} \leq \theta$

$$\text{Clearly, } F(0)=0;\ F(\bar{\theta})=1,\ F'(\theta)=\frac{1}{\bar{\theta}}\ \forall\, \theta \in (0,\bar{\theta}];\ F(\theta)=\frac{\theta}{\bar{\theta}} \tag{2}$$

It is also assumed for simplification that a consumer either consumes one unit of X or does not consume at all.

Evidently, the θ-consumer buys X iff $\theta \geq p/s$ (3)

The market demand for X may, therefore, be given by

$$D(p,s) = \left\{1 - F\left(\frac{p}{s}\right)\right\} n = \left(1 - \frac{p}{s\bar{\theta}}\right) n \tag{4}$$

Let us now assume that a copyright producer is a monopoly producer of X. Given the cost parameters relating to development and marketing of X, life cycle of X, discount rate, and insignificant marginal cost which is assumed to be zero let the annualized cost of production be $\bar{c}$.

The monopolist's profit maximization project may be written as

$$\max_{p}\ \pi = \left(1 - \frac{p}{s\bar{\theta}}\right) np - \bar{c}$$

The above maximization exercise yields the optimum price

$$p_m = \frac{s\bar{\theta}}{2} \tag{5}$$

The maximized profit, which can be calculated by substituting (5) in the profit function π, is

$$\pi_m = \frac{ns\overline{\theta}}{4} - \overline{c} \tag{6}$$

Presumably, $\pi_m \geq 0 \Rightarrow \frac{ns\overline{\theta}}{4} \geq \overline{c}$ (7)

By using (5) in (4), we get the result that copyright producer as a monopolist decides to cater to only half the potential market.

Consumer surplus corresponding to this equilibrium is given by

$$CS_m = \int_{\theta/2}^{\overline{\theta}} (\theta s - p_m) F'(\theta) n d\theta$$

$$= \frac{n}{\overline{\theta}} \int_{\theta/2}^{\overline{\theta}} \left(\theta s - \frac{\theta s}{2} \right) d\theta$$

$$= \frac{ns\overline{\theta}}{8} \tag{8}$$

From (6) and (8) social surplus works out to be

$$SS_m = CS_m + \pi_m = \frac{3ns\overline{\theta}}{8} - \overline{c} \tag{9}$$

However, once X has been developed and marketed it is technically possible for anybody to make copies of the product without incurring the fixed cost $\overline{c}$. Since MC ≅ 0, any positive price would bring profit. The copyright producer cannot, however, be priced out of the market since the pirated version of quality s_p is inferior to the original version (i.e., $s > s_p > 0$) and some high end consumers will continue to buy from the copyright producer. Under this situation entry of commercial pirates is a logical conclusion. In absence of monitoring the copyright producer has three options—(i) to accommodate the pirates, (ii) to prevent entry by making X copy-protected, and (iii) not to bring in the product at all. The option the copyright producer will take is the option which costs the least to her. Accommodating pirates will involve cost since the pirates take away a part of her monopoly market; the copy-protection option involves cost of investment in copy protection technology; and not participating in the market costs her normal as well as supernormal profit. It is, therefore, important that we weigh each option separately and then compare the costs to predict the reaction of the copyright producer to the spectre of piracy. It is also important to calculate the resultant social surpluses.

(i) **Accommodating the pirates:** Entry of commercial pirates destroys the monopoly nature of the market for X by splitting it into two segments – the copyright producer catering the original X version of quality s to the high end consumers, and the pirates catering the pirated version of quality s_p to the low end consumers. The choice of the θ-consumer is given by the following:

Necessary and sufficient condition for buying the original version (s):

$$(a)\ \theta s - p > \theta s_p - p_p \Rightarrow \theta > \frac{(p - p_p)}{(s - s_p)},\ (b)\ \theta > \frac{p}{s} \tag{10}$$

Necessary condition for buying the pirated version (s_p):

$$(a)\ \theta < \frac{(p - p_p)}{(s - s_p)},\ (b)\ \theta > \frac{p_p}{s_p} \tag{11}$$

Lemma 1: For pirates to operate it is required that $\frac{(p - p_p)}{(s - s_p)} > \frac{p}{s} > \frac{p_p}{s_p}$

Proof: If $\frac{p}{s} \leq \frac{p_p}{s_p}$, then $\forall \theta$

$$\theta - \frac{p}{s} \geq \theta - \frac{p_p}{s_p} \Rightarrow (\theta s - p) \geq (\theta s_p - p_p)\frac{s}{s_p} \Rightarrow (\theta s - p) > (\theta s_p - p_p)$$

This precludes existence of pirates. Since existence of pirates is presumed,

$$\frac{p}{s} > \frac{p_p}{s_p} \Rightarrow ps_p > p_p s \Rightarrow ps - ps_p < ps - p_p s \Rightarrow p(s - s_p) < s(p - p_p)$$

$$\Rightarrow \frac{(p - p_p)}{(s - s_p)} > \frac{p}{s}\ \blacksquare$$

From (10), (11), and Lemma 1 the following demand functions for s and s_p can be derived:

$$D_s = \left\{1 - \frac{(p - p_p)}{\overline{\theta}(s - s_p)}\right\}n \tag{12}$$

$$D_p = \left\{ \frac{(p - p_p)}{(s - s_p)} - \frac{p_p}{s_p} \right\} \frac{n}{\overline{\theta}} \tag{13}$$

Since the pirates operate in the competitive fringe the equilibrium p_p is the MC of production. Therefore, equilibrium $p_p, p_p^e \cong 0$ (14)

By backward induction, the copyright producer's problem is to

$$\max_{p} \ \pi_m = \left\{ 1 - \frac{p}{\overline{\theta}(s - s_p)} \right\} np - \overline{c}$$

First order condition yields

$$p_m^* = \frac{\overline{\theta}(s - s_p)}{2} \tag{15}$$

$$\pi_m^* = \frac{(s - s_p) n\overline{\theta}}{4} - \overline{c} \tag{16}$$

Comparing (15) and (16) with (5) and (6) we can conclude that accommodating pirates implies lower price and profit for the copyright producer compared to the monopoly levels. She, however, continues to have the same clientele size of $\frac{n}{2} [\because (12) \& (15), (4) \& (5)]$.

Pirates on their part earns zero supernormal profit, i.e., $\pi_p^e = 0$ (17)

Therefore, producers' surplus under piracy is less than the producer's surplus under monopoly $[\because (6) \& (16), (17)]$

Consumers' surplus under piracy can be expressed as

$$CS_p = \frac{n}{\overline{\theta}} \left[\int_{\overline{\theta}/2}^{\overline{\theta}} \left(\theta s - \frac{\overline{\theta}(s - s_p)}{2} \right) d\theta + \int_0^{\overline{\theta}/2} \theta s_p d\theta \right] = \frac{n\overline{\theta}(s + 3s_p)}{8} \tag{18}$$

Therefore, piracy induced social surplus turns out to be

$$SS_p = \pi_m^* + \pi_p^e + CS_p = \frac{n\overline{\theta}(3s + s_p)}{8} - \overline{c} > SS_m \tag{19}$$

Piracy, therefore, not only raises the consumer surplus but also the social surplus from the monopoly equilibrium level $[\because (8) \& (9), (18), (19)]$

(ii) **Entry deterring investment:** Instead of accommodating the piracy fringe the copyright producer may try to make the original version of X copy protected by investing in copy protection technology. Even if we disregard the probability of copy protection code being cracked by some pirate, the annualized cost of copy protection is significant. Let k > 0 denote this additional cost to the copyright producer. The copyright producer in this case continues to have a monopoly outcome with profit reduced by k. The reduced profit is given by modifying the indirect profit function (6)

$$\pi_{cp} = \frac{ns\bar{\theta}}{4} - \bar{c} - k \tag{20}$$

The corresponding social surplus works out to be

$$SS_{cp} = \frac{3n\bar{\theta}s}{8} - \bar{c} - k \tag{21}$$

(iii) From indirect profit functions (6), (16) and (20) we get the following viability conditions for accommodating pirates and fighting pirates respectively:

$$\pi_m^* = \frac{(s - s_p)n\bar{\theta}}{4} - \bar{c} \geq 0 \Rightarrow \pi_m \geq \frac{ns_p\bar{\theta}}{4} \tag{22}$$

$$\pi_{cp} = \frac{ns\bar{\theta}}{4} - \bar{c} - k \geq 0 \Rightarrow \pi_m \geq k \tag{23}$$

When none of (22) and (23) is fulfilled the copyright producer will fail to survive either by fighting or by accommodating the pirates. The only sub-game perfect Nash equilibrium (SPNE) under this condition involves the copyright producer not bringing the product to the market at all. Needless to say, social surplus is zero.

Actions of the Copyright producer

It is quite clear from conditions (22) and (23) above that the SPNE is dictated by $min\left\{\pi_m, \frac{ns_p\bar{\theta}}{4}, k\right\}$. If π_m is the minimum, the product X will not be developed at all if there is no effective copyright protection, since $\pi_m^* < 0, \pi_{cp} < 0$. If $\frac{ns_p\bar{\theta}}{4}$ is the lowest, then in absence of copyright protection the copyright producer would produce X without trying to make it copy-protected. Only when k is the lowest the copyright producer will make any effort to invest in copy protection.

It can be easily shown from conditions (22) and (23) that higher values of s, n and $\overline{\theta}$, ceteris paribus, raise the likelihood of X getting developed. When the market is large and/or there is a wide spread of θ among the consumers, and/or quality of the original version is high the copyright producer is more likely to survive on her own. The values of the parameters $\overline{c}$, k, and s_p on the other hand work to the opposite effect. That cost of investments is a dampener on production can hardly be called a startling revelation, but that a wider spread between s and s_p encourages accommodation is a more interesting observation. The reason why the music industry the world over cry much hoarser than, say, the producers of antivirus software may be found in this result. However, monopoly is the best result for the copyright producer under any circumstances.

Policy issues

The raison d'être for copyright protection is encouragement of innovation and creation of new products. In the process monopoly is created. One may argue that this is the price the society pays for product variation. In this model the social price of product variation is shown in terms of lower social surplus under monopoly compared to the scenario when monopoly is dented by pirates. The scenario is even worse when the copyright producer reacts by investing in copy protection devises, because that is a net waste to the society. With the help of this model it can also be argued that in certain cases the society can have product variation and yet need not suffer monopoly. In the previous section it was argued that when $\frac{ns_p\overline{\theta}}{4} = min\left\{\pi_m, \frac{ns_p\overline{\theta}}{4}, k\right\}$ a non-monopoly equilibrium involving unfettered piracy obtains with social outcome more desirable than under monopoly. However, it needs to be seen whether a still better result is possible in absence of, but under threat of, piracy. When $\pi_m = min\left\{\pi_m, \frac{ns_p\overline{\theta}}{4}, k\right\}$ the SPNE is the classic case warranting copyright protection, because in this case there is no production in absence of any monitoring of piracy. The question is, however, about the degree of monitoring. The copyright producer is always expected to demand a protection level that would ensure her the monopoly market. The objective of the Copyright Authority is, however, to choose a protection level to maximize the social surplus subject to the constraint that the copyright producer earns her normal profit. The protection is measured by the degree of monitoring copyright infringement. Monitoring in turn is measured by expected penalty of piracy, which may be assumed to be a linear function of quantity of pirated X produced. The marginal cost of piracy can, therefore, be treated as a policy variable. Let this marginal cost of piracy be denoted by *mc*.

With this modification about the nature of marginal cost of the pirates the assumption of near-zero marginal cost is now discarded. As a result optimal price and the indirect profit function of the copyright producer given by (15) and (16) are modified in the following generalized form

$$p_m^* = \frac{\bar{\theta}(s - s_p) + mc}{2} \tag{15'}$$

$$\pi_m^* = \frac{n\{(s - s_p)\bar{\theta} + mc\}^2}{4(s - s_p)\bar{\theta}} - \bar{c} \tag{16'}$$

subject to Lemma 1, which implies $mc < \dfrac{\bar{\theta}s_p(s - s_p)}{(2s - s_p)}$ (24)

Since at $mc \cong 0$, $\pi_m^* < 0$ as well as $\pi_{cp} < 0$ when $\pi_m = min\left\{\pi_m, \dfrac{ns_p\bar{\theta}}{4}, k\right\}$ the copyright producer cannot survive unless the Copyright Authority raises *mc* for the pirates to increase the RHS of (16′) to a non-negative value. The Copyright Authority on its part has to weigh two options against each other. One option is to go by the demand by the copyright producer to clamp at least the minimum *mc* on the pirates which is just too high for the pirates to command any market at a price equal to their *mc* when the copyright producer charges her monopoly price. Putting the monopoly price from equation (5) and substituting p_p by its equilibrium value *mc* in the pirates' demand function (13) and then setting the latter equal to zero gives the required value of $mc = \dfrac{\bar{\theta}s_p}{2}$. The other option is to choose a somewhat lower value of *mc*. It is verifiable that setting $mc = \dfrac{\bar{\theta}s_p(s - s_p)}{(2s - s_p)} < \dfrac{\bar{\theta}s_p}{2}$ keeping in mind condition (24) is just enough to nudge the pirates out. Yet it does not allow the copyright producer to charge the monopoly price although she is now able to raise her profit level π_m^* to the maximum extent possible under piracy threat. If this is enough to turn her fate around, i.e., if the profit expression (16′) turns non-negative, then it can be shown that at a monitoring level $mc = \frac{\bar{\theta}s_p(s-s_p)}{(2s-s_p)} < \frac{\bar{\theta}s_p}{2}$ the resultant social surplus works out to be higher than what obtains under monopoly:

$$SS_G = \frac{(3-2\rho)}{2(2-\rho)^2} n\bar{\theta}s - \bar{c} > \frac{3}{8} n\bar{\theta}s - \bar{c} = SS_m; \text{ where } s_p = \rho s,\ \rho \in (0,\ 1) \qquad (25)^2$$

Interestingly, the piracy preventive monitoring level $mc = \frac{\bar{\theta}s_p(s-s_p)}{(2s-s_p)}$ also scores over unfettered piracy on the same social criterion, since

$$SS_G = \frac{(3-2\rho)}{2(2-\rho)^2} n\bar{\theta}s - \bar{c} > \frac{(3+\rho)}{8} n\bar{\theta}s - \bar{c} = SS_p. \qquad (26)^3$$

Combining (19), (25) and (26), $SS_G > SS_p > SS_m$ (27)

Piracy is better than monopoly, but this is not the best of social outcomes. Piracy needs to be banished, but it is best to keep its threat breathing down the neck of the copyright producer, because monopoly is the worst social outcome. The copyright producer must be protected, but she must not get the protection she demands unless that is absolutely necessity for her survival.

References

Banerjee, D.S., Banerjee, T. and Raychoudhuri, A., 2008. "Optimal enforcement and anti-copying strategies to counter copyright infringement", *Japanese Economic Review,* 59, (4), 519-535.

Banerjee, D.S., 2006. "Lobbying and commercial software piracy", *European Journal of Political Economy*, 22, 139-155.

Joshua Slive and Dan Bernhardt, 1998. "Pirated for Profit", *Canadian Journal of Economics*, Canadian Economics Association, Vol. 31(4), pages 886-899, November.

---

[2] Appendix 1

[3] Appendix 2

Oz Shy and Jacques-Françlois Thisse, 1999. "A Strategic Approach to Software Protection", *Journal of Economics and Management Strategy*, Blackwell Publishing, Vol. 8(2), pages 163-190, 06.

Poddar, S, 2005. "Network Externality and Commercial Software Piracy", *Working paper* # 0516, Dept. of Economics, National University of Singapore.

Appendix 1

Putting $mc = \dfrac{\bar{\theta} s_p (s - s_p)}{(2s - s_p)}$ in (16′),

$$\pi_m^* = \frac{s^2 n\bar{\theta}(s - s_p)}{(2s - s_p)^2} - \bar{c} = \frac{4(1-\rho)}{(2-\rho)^2} \cdot \frac{n\bar{\theta}s}{4} - \bar{c} < \frac{n\bar{\theta}s}{4} - \bar{c} = \pi_m$$

$$CS_G = \frac{n}{\bar{\theta}} \int_{p_m^*/s}^{\bar{\theta}} (\theta s - p_m^*) d\theta = \frac{n}{\bar{\theta}} \int_{\frac{(1-\rho)\bar{\theta}}{(2-\rho)}}^{\bar{\theta}} \left(\theta s - \frac{(1-\rho)s\bar{\theta}}{(2-\rho)} \right) d\theta = \frac{n\bar{\theta}s}{2(2-\rho)^2}$$

Therefore,

$$SS_G = \pi_m^* + CS_G = \frac{(3-2\rho)}{2(2-\rho)^2} n\bar{\theta}s - \bar{c} > \frac{3}{8} n\bar{\theta}s - \bar{c} = SS_m$$

Appendix 2

We have $SS_G = \dfrac{(3-2\rho)}{2(2-\rho)^2} n\bar{\theta}s - \bar{c}$ from (25)

and $SS_p = \dfrac{n\bar{\theta}(3s + s_p)}{8} - \bar{c} = \dfrac{(3+\rho)}{8} n\bar{\theta}s - \bar{c}$ from (19) and (25)

Again, $\dfrac{(3-2\rho)}{2(2-\rho)^2} > \dfrac{(3+\rho)}{8}$ $[\because \rho \in (0,1)]$

$\therefore\ SS_G > SS_p$ ■

Disparity in Manufacturing Industries among Major Indian States: The Importance of Fiscal Reforms during Reform Period

Debraj Das and Debnarayan Sarker

This paper is an attempt to present the disparities of state-level performance of manufacturing industry on some key variables and tries to examine whether fiscal reforms play a significant role for such a disparity among major Indian states during reform period. The study suggests that Indian states which could contribute to higher economic and administrative reforms during reform period by various fiscal measures did gain the boon of industrial achievements. So, in order to gain industrial uplift, the fiscal reforms of a state must help raising the income level of the particular state reflecting thereby to develop her economy by receiving the fruits of industrial development.

As is well known, the economic policy environment for industries in Indian states since 1991 has undergone unprecedented changes and has become much more competitive than past. Such a change has been effective mainly due to removal of industrial licensing system, drastic reduction in the number of industries reserved exclusively for public sector, treatment for FDI on par with domestic private investment and removal of restrictions on monopolies. As a result of such a change it is now well established that the inter-state disparities in the growth of gross state domestic product (GSDP) have increased in the post economic reform period beginning from the early nineties when compared to the eighties. In general, the richer states have grown faster than the poorer ones (Ahluwalia 2000; Dev and Ravi, 2003; Bhattacharya and Sakthivel, 2004). The GSDP from secondary sector during the post-reform period is one of the important factors for higher variability of inter-state disparities. The richer states have higher industrial growth during the post-reform period than the poorer ones due, mainly, to higher performance of manufacturing industries at state-level. This paper is an attempt to present the disparities of state-level performance of manufacturing industry on some key variables and tries to examine as to whether fiscal reforms play an important role for such disparity among major Indian states during reform period.

The paper is organized as follows. Part I presents discussions on Industrial performance in major Indian states and the profit efficiency based on two important factors of Industrial performance among those states. The underlying reason influencing such industrial performance most among major Indian states during the period of economic reforms appears in Part II. Part III concludes.

PART I

Industrial Performance of Indian States

The performance of the industries can be assessed, among others, by some key variables viz. employment, number of factories and value added. The percentage share of all these key variables to all India level have significantly increased to some of the states during the phase of economic reforms vis-à-vis other Indian states. The states which have experienced better performance in net value added and employment have been afforded to take the advantages of economic reforms through providing a series of reforms they made within their own states.

Table 8.1: Performance of Manufacturing Industry in Major Indian States

(For the span of 30 years)

States	*Percentage Shares of Major Indian States to All India*								
	No. of Factories			*Persons Employed*			*Net Value Added*		
	1977–78	*1988–89*	*2004–05*	*1977–78*	*1988–89*	*2004–05*	*1977–78*	*1988–89*	*2004–05*
A.P.	7.84	13.73	11.42	7.09	9.38	11.88	4.76	5.26	6.13
Assam	3.23	1.58	1.25	1.99	1.49	1.53	2.37	1.09	1.43
Bihar	4.27	3.31	2.41	5.92	4.9	2.56	5.17	7.44	6.8
Gujarat	10.04	10.67	9.97	8.31	8.72	9.2	10.04	9.78	13.86
Haryana	2.48	2.65	3.18	1.97	2.94	4.07	2.62	2.91	4.5
H.P.	0.46	0.25	0.48	.30	.67	0.51	0.5	0.86	.84
Karnataka	5.75	5.43	5.57	5.03	5.14	6.53	4.93	4.69	7.9
Kerala	4.41	2.95	4.03	3.96	3.02	4.16	2.73	2.74	1.56
M.P.	4.32	3.49	2.22	4.19	4.09	2.48	4.5	4.95	2.14
Maharastra	17.35	14.53	13.87	17.78	15.67	12.34	24.93	23.72	19.74
Orissa	0.99	1.37	1.28	1.76	2.0	1.77	1.97	2.55	2.33
Punjab	3.36	5.76	5.56	2.38	4.91	4.69	2.39	3.09	2.23
Rajasthan	1.91	3.04	4.25	2.19	2.99	3.15	2.39	2.55	2.53
TamilNadu	10.41	12.59	15.44	9.54	11.59	15.86	10.09	10.86	8.3
U.P.	9.68	9.04	7.03	9.97	9.77	6.86	6.38	8.59	5.5
W.B.	10.10	5.21	4.48	15.01	9.77	6.33	12.15	6.34	4.06

Source: Statistical Abstract.

Table 8.1, representing percentage share of major Indian states to all India level: net value added, employment and number of factories in manufacturing industries, shows that during the period of economic reform Gujarat, Karnataka, Andhra Pradesh, Haryana, Assam, Himachal Pradesh and Rajasthan registered better performance than others, when performance of all variables are taken together .Although the percentage share of number of factories of all India level registered some decrease, but with regard to net value added and employment their performance shows a significant increase in their shares. State-wise, for Punjab, net value added shows some declining sign, whereas for other variable Punjab's position proves significant progress .Turning to Maharastra, one may find that although its share for all the variables shows some declining figures to its share in relation to all India level during reform period, the highest share of net value added is still occupied by Maharastra in 2004-05, the second highest share being registered in employment and factories. The poor industrial performance in all the variables is registered by West Bengal, Madhya Pradesh, Uttar Pradesh, old Bihar and Orissa. But Orissa did much better than all other states which performed badly during the reform period.

Significantly as regards the other poorly performed states except West Bengal and U.P. are concerned, the historical industrial performance of all these states is poor during the past as well as during the present. Turning to the performance of West Bengal, the tradition of industrial development in manufacturing sector that West Bengal registered during the past has significantly deteriorated during the current years. Such a decline which started in the late 70's has been going on for this long time. It is worth mentioning that there is no other Indian states which did register such a decline during over 3 decades. West Bengal was the second major industrial states in terms of value added and number of employment, registering third highest position in the case of number of factories during 1977–78, when the present left front government came into power. However during 28 years of their ruling starting from 1977-78 to 2004-05, the West Bengal's industrial performance has been steeped down to the 8th position among major Indian states in the performance of all the variables namely number of factories, net value added and employment. The declining trend of all these key variables not only registered pre-reform period, but also worked out during post economic reform.

The percentage share of West Bengal to all India level with respect to number of factories, net value added and employment in manufacturing industry decreased from 10.10 to 4.48 percent, 12.15 to 4.06 per cent and 15.01 to 6.33 percent respectively for 28 years from 1977-78 to 2004-05.Most importantly, the rate of decline for all the performance variables during their 28 years period is the highest for West Bengal of all major Indian states. If one compares the industrial performance during pre reform to post-reform period of existing left front regime, one may find that the decline of all the variables is much higher during the pre-reform period than the post-reform period.

But if one compares relative performance of manufacturing industry between U.P. and W.B, the performance of all these variables for U.P. is not so poor as West Bengal. The relative position of U.P. during 28 years starting from 1977-78 to 2004-05 has more or less unchanged among all Indian states.

The data relating to performance at State level Public Sector Enterprise of manufacturing industries (Table 8.2) are also in conformity with the findings of table 8.1. It shows that West Bengal has registered the worst performance of state level public sector enterprise among major Indian states. The performances of other major states are much better than that of West Bengal state.

Table 8.2: Performance of State-Level Public Sector Enterprise

	Proportion of loss-making PSEs (%)	*Proportion of PSEs with negative net worth (%)*	*Rate of return on capital (average)*
Andhra Pradesh	15	14.8	10.0
Assam	17	20.9	–16.4
Bihar	70	11.1	–7.7
Gujarat	39	17.6	–8.9
Haryana	59	13.8	5.0
Himachal Pradesh	62	23.8	5.7
Karnataka	41	7.3	31.2
Kerala	61	14	–15.3
Madhya Pradesh	33	14.3	2.2
Maharastra	68	20.7	–4.6
Orissa	70	21.7	–35.0
Punjab	44	15.8	–12.0
Rajasthan	38	20.8	20.6
Tamil Nadu	53	29.4	–1.6
Uttar Pradesh	62	17.0	–29.9
West Bengal	72	44.2	–45.2

Source: OECD (2007) analysis of data from the Comptroller and Auditor General.

Efficiency of Industrial Performance

Which state (states) did gain higher profit efficiency in manufacturing industry among major Indian states? While examining this issue we consider three main key variables: employment, productive capital and net value added. We examined the industrial performance of labour cost and productive capital on net value added during reform period based on three time points 1978–79, 1988–89 and 2003–04 (Table 8.3).

The calculation of profit efficiency[1] seems to be essential as to know whether the richer Indian states which gain the fruits of industrialization could efficiently use the two most important factors-labour cost and productive capital-efficiently as compared with the poor Indian states which failed to gain the fruits of industrialization. Table 8.3 shows that except Andhra Pradesh all rich Indian states which did gain the fruits of such industrialization received higher profit efficiency during reform period, particularly during 1988–89 and 2003–04. Andhra Pradesh did fail to receive higher profit efficiency because of the fact that the incidence of her net value added were much below than the increment of her productive use of capital and labour.But West Bengal is also an exception because of the fact that despite being middle income state she looses both in quantitative as well as qualitative upliftment in industria-lization during reform period.

Table 8.3: Measurement of Profit Efficiency among major Indian States

(Using DEA Analysis)

States	*1978–79*	*1988–89*	*2003–04*
Andhra Pradesh	.58	.61	.50
Assam	.69	.75	.70
Bihar	.85	.77	0.62
Gujarat	.86	.80	.92
NBS Haryana	.79	.71	.75
Himachal Pradesh	.68	.73	.81
Karnataka	.72	.78	.84
Kerala	.57	.90	.72
Madhya Pradesh	.70	.75	.80
Maharastra	.78	.83	.86
Orissa	.56	.51	.46
Punjab	.54	.55	.82
Rajasthan	.56	.54	.76
Tamil Nadu	.95	.75	.80
Uttar Pradesh	.57	.58	.89
West Bengal	.84	.68	.65

PART II

What are the significant reasons as to why the poorer states loose in gaining industrial boon in relation to the richer ones during economic reform period? The economic survey report of OECD countries (in a study of 20 major Indian states) states that Indian states which could contribute to higher economic and administrative reforms by various measures did gain the boon of industrial achievements in these respective Indian states, where West Bengal registered the least fiscal reforms of all[2]. OECD (2007) report also argue, "to begin with the process of closing the gaps in economic performance across states, the relatively restrictive states need to improve their regulatory environment so as to become more competitive and productive" (p. 94). One may argue that already existing better infrastructure that prevailed before reforms is the most significant reasons for the industrial achievements of richer Indian states. As is well known, West Bengal is one of the middle income states like TN, Kerala, Karnataka, but before 1980 for infrastructural development she tops almost all Indian states. West Bengal registered second major industrial states in terms of net value added and number of workers employed and third in terms of number of factories. But as mentioned earlier, the industrial performance of West Bengal has been stepped down to the 8th position among Indian states during economic reform period. The fact is that the states which registered better industrial performance during reform period mainly due to higher fiscal reform did also register better infrastructural uplift during reform period.

The other factors responsible for inter-state disparities in industrial front are the industrial licensing system, drastic reduction in the number of industries reserved exclusively for public sector, treatment for FDI on par with domestic private investment etc. As a result of such a change it is now well established that the inter-state disparities in the growth of gross state domestic product (GSDP) have increased in the post economic reform period beginning from the early nineties when compared to the eighties. But the most significant force behind industrial uplift for richer Indian states during reform period is the higher economic and administrative reforms that they introduced by various fiscal measures.

Implication of Reforms on some Vital Areas among Major Indian States

Why did the richer Indian states, which did better performance in industrial uplift, execute their reform measures which did help the boon of such industrialization during reform period? This paper also points out to some of the vital areas of such implications:

Strikes and Lockouts

One of the significant factors regarding the industrial set back for West Bengal state is strike and lockouts which almost appear owing to the positive incentive of West Bengal left front government. Table 8.4 shows the statement of man days lost due to industrial disputes (strikes and lockouts) which did face the high incidence of man-days lost due to strikes and lock-outs during 1979-2005 among major Indian states. As may be seen in table 8.4, for a single year in 2005, about 3 crores (2,74,65,318) man days were lost for strikes and lockouts. West Bengal alone shares approximately 68.94 per cent man days lost out of all man days in India during 2005.If one compares the figure before economic reform and during economic reform period during the regime of present left front government one may find that in 1979, West Bengal alone shared 41.22 per cent of total man days lost in India due to strikes and lock outs. Interestingly, the states having higher incidence of man days lost due to strikes and lock outs except West Bengal account for 35.92 per cent approximately if the figures of 8 states are combined together in 1979. Worthwhile to mention that in 1979, the industrial performance of all Indian states except Maharastra and Tamil Nadu was much worse than that of West Bengal state. Also important is that during ten years period (1979–1989) before economic reform the proportion of man days lost for strikes and lock outs were more or less same in West Bengal state, the share of West Bengal being 41.18 percent of total, where for the rest the combined figure works at to 48.7 per cent of total approximately. What it implies is that during pre-reform period from 1979 to 1989 the combined figure of man days lost for 8 major Indian states were more or less nearer to the figure of West Bengal state alone. But interestingly, the data during 1989-2005 shows that 8 major Indian states register two fundamental changes in industrial performance (1) all these states made higher industrial progress in relation to West Bengal. (Table 8.1), (2) The politics of man days lost due to strikes and lockouts almost came to an end in all these states, because the combined man days lost to all these states except West Bengal is approximately 10.45 per cent of total man days lost of India in 2005, whereas in 1989, a period of 16 years back, their combined contribution was 35.92 per cent approximately. But in 2005 the man days lost in West Bengal alone register 68.94 per cent approximately of total man days lost in India. (more than two third man days lost in Indian states). These results, however, reveal that during the reform period the man days lost for lock outs and strikes significantly increases in West Bengal, whereas they decreases substantially in those states which made higher progress in industrial scene than West Bengal during reform period. The state of West Bengal, among others, did fail to have the fruits of industrial progress because of the fact that (one of the most significant reasons) the government of West Bengal did not execute her reform policy in minimizing industrial dispute from strikes and lock-outs: rather she did execute her positive role in augmenting the same.

Table 8.4: Figure of Strikes and Lock-Outs in some Major States of India

(Percentage Shares of Major Indian States to All India)

States	*1979*	*1989*	*2005*
Andhra Pradesh	1.51	16.59	2.49
Gujarat	1.24	1.42	0.42
Haryana	1.96	2.09	1.79
Karnataka	2.16	0.97	1.17
Maharastra	6.79	14.95	1.78
Punjab	0.17	1.90	0.10
Tamil Nadu	19.17	9.69	2.38
Uttar Pradesh	2.92	1.09	0.32
West Bengal	41.22	41.18	68.94

Source: Labour Bureau (Simla): *labourbureau.nic.in*

Foreign Direct Investment

Foreign Direct Investment is one of the significant factors for industrialization. The Indian states which attracted higher foreign direct investment could do it mainly because of positive role of reforms by state governments.

None but five Indian states namely Gujrat, Karnataka, Maharastra, A.P. and Tamil Nadu have higher incidence of foreign direct investment during reform period. (Table 8.5) If one examines state-wise data regarding the performance of foreign direct investment during reform period, one may have some important features.

With regard to per capita FDI is concerned (Table 8.5) seven Indian states–Haryana, Himachal Pradesh, Karnataka, Maharastra, Tamil Nadu, Gujarat, Andhra Pradesh—have higher incidence of per capita FDI during the reform period (1991–2003). It however implies that all high income and middle income group of states except Punjab, which belongs to high income group, and Kerala and West Bengal, which belong to middle income group of states, under major Indian states belonging to general category have higher incidence of FDI during reform period. Importantly, despite the fact that Punjab had lower FDI during reform period, their internal flow of productive capital was much stronger than West Bengal and Kerala. The failure of West Bengal and Kerala in attracting FDI due to their anti-imperialist role against FDI by the left front government in those two states indicating a negative role of fiscal policies by the latter. Worthwhile to mention that OECD (2007) points out 'with relatively more liberal states receiving virtually all of India's FDI flows' (p. 93).

Table 8.5: State-wise Break up of Amount of FDI Approved by Government

States	*Amt. of FDI Approved (1991–2003)*	*% Share of Total*	*Per Capita FDI (₹)1991-2003 (average)*
A.P.	134025.61	4.61	136.94
Assam	14.95	0	0.05
Bihar	8842.20	.3	6.79
Gujarat	188184.47	6.47	303.02
Haryana	38634.11	1.33	153.27
H.P.	11740.17	.4	154.48
Karnataka	239969.98	8.25	360.75
Kerala	15457.91	0.53	37.76
M.P.	99041.29	3.41	99.69
Maharastra	507121.41	17.44	424.37
Orissa	82239.13	2.83	65.85
Punjab	24226.50	0.83	82.53
Rajasthan	30072.42	1.03	44.92
TamilNadu	248104.83	8.53	312.72
U.P.	50401.78	1.73	24.19
W.B.	92606.18	3.18	93.70

Source: SIA. Newsletter Annual Issue 2000 and 2002 and SIA Monthly Newsletters from January to December 2003.

Electrification

Low per capita consumption of power is also one of the vital factors in some major Indian states (namely Assam, Bihar, Kerala, Orissa, U.P. and West Bengal) for lower incidence of industrialization (Table 8.6). This is almost due to the lack of reform policies (economic and administrative) by state governments in almost all these states. It is said that to build up physical infrastructure like electricity, both FDI and internal private investments need fiscal reforms by the state governments to attract these investments within those states. However those states failed to execute such reform measures in attracting these investments.

Availability of higher incidence of physical infrastructure like electricity is also a pre-requisite for higher incidence of industrialization. Poor physical infrastructure of electricity is a reflection of poor investment climate which fails to improve state's comparative advantage for industrialization.

Table 8.6: State-wise Per Capita Consumption of Power

States	*Per Capita Consumption of Power*	
	1991	*2003*
A.P.	245.22	672.6
Assam	93.53	160
Bihar	110.07	274.6
Gujarat	469.33	1192.9
Haryana	400.4	997.1
H.P.	208.91	598.7
Karnataka	295.99	611.2
Kerala	186.45	377.5
M.P.	247.38	598.1
Maharastra	410.87	848
Orissa	270.72	470.2
Punjab	605.81	1227.4
Rajasthan	201.48	566.1
Tamil Nadu	323.03	815.3
U.P.	165.85	389.9
W.B.	146.18	366.5

Source: CMIE Infrastructure.

Telephone

States having higher incidence of industrial units have higher infrastructure of telephone during reform period (Table 8.7). Kerala is an exception in this regard: despite having lower incidence of industrialization during reform period, the number of telephone per 100 person has significantly increased during this period. The establishment of physical infrastructure like telephone also depends on state reform policies. Obviously, states registering higher incidence of industrial units executed more favorable policies which help to augment the infrastructure of telephone and so they gain the fruits of industrialization. What it seems to imply is that to begin with the process of closing the gaps in economic performance across states, the relatively restrictive states need to improve their regulatory environment so as to become more competitive and productive.

Table 8.7: Telephones per 100 persons among Indian States (during 1991–2003)

States	*Telephones per 100 persons*	
	1991	*2003*
A.P.	0.48	7.85
Assam	0.17	2.13
Bihar	0.11	1.84
Gujarat	1.05	10.14
Haryana	0.57	8.38
H.P.	0.57	10.14
Karnataka	0.68	9.46
Kerala	0.8	14.87
M.P.	0.26	2.81
Maharastra	1.26	8
Orissa	0.19	2.95
Punjab	0.95	17.33
Rajasthan	0.32	4.5
Tamil Nadu	0.78	8.54
U.P.	0.21	4.03
W.B.	0.46	2.18

Source: CMIE Infrastructure.

PART III

Conclusions

This study lends credence to the fact that the richer states have higher industrial growth during the post-reform period than the poorer ones due mainly to higher performance of manufacturing industries at state-level both quantitatively and qualitatively. What are the significant reasons as to why the poorer states loose in gaining industrial boon in relation to the richer ones during economic reform period? The study, however, suggests that Indian states which could contribute to higher economic and administrative reforms by various measures during economic reform period did gain the boon of industrial achievements. One may argue that already existing better infrastructure that prevailed before reforms is the most significant reasons for the industrial achievements of richer Indian states. As is well known, West Bengal is one of the middle income states like TN, Kerala, and Karnataka; but before 1980, for infrastructural development she tops over almost all Indian states. West Bengal registered second major industrial states in terms of net value added and number of workers employed and third in terms of number of factories. But the industrial performance of West Bengal has been stepped down to the 8th position among Indian states during economic reform period. Although other factors—like industrial licensing system, industries reserved exclusively for public sector, treatment for FDI on par with domestic private investment—are responsible for industrial disparity among Indian states, the most important fact is that the states which registered better industrial performance during reform period mainly due to higher fiscal reform did also register better infrastructural uplift during reform period. OECD(2007) report also argue, "to begin with the process of closing the gaps in economic performance across states, the relatively restrictive states need to improve their regulatory environment so as to become more competitive and productive"(p.94). So, the fiscal reforms of a state introduced by various economic and administrative reforms must help raising the income level of the particular state reflecting thereby to develop her economy which might gain the fruit of industrial development.

Notes

1. **Profit efficiency analysis:** In econometric applications one specifies some explicit form of the production, cost, or profit function to represent the benchmark technology for efficiency measurement. The maximum profit is the profit function underlying what may be considered as the best practice techniques utilized by a given group of firms. The interest of the sample firms (here, major Indian States) is focused on ascertaining the highest profit using the best practice technique at the firm level given the level of technology and the feasibility of input-output bundle chosen. We use the following method to analysis profit efficiency using DEA.

   In econometric applications one specifies some explicit form of the production, cost, or profit function to represent bench-mark technology for efficiency measurement. We also measure the profit efficiency of major Indian states based on three financial performance indicators (labour cost and productive capital on net value added). The procedure of its measure is as follow:

   The method of data envelopment analysis introduced by Charnes *et. al.* (1978) and further extended to non-constant returns technologies by Banker, Charnes and Cooper (BCC) (1984) and Charnes *et. al.* (1985) provides a way to construct the production possibility set from an observed data set of input-output bundles.

   Suppose that (X^j ,Y^j) is the input-output bundle observed for firm j (j = 1, 2,……., N). Clearly, these input-output bundles are all feasible. Then the smallest production possibility set satisfying the assumption of convexity and free disposability that includes these observed bundles is

$$S = \{(X,Y): X \geq \sum_{j=1}^{N} \lambda_j X^j; Y \leq \sum_{j=1}^{N} \lambda_j X^j; \sum_{j=1}^{N} \lambda_j = 1; \lambda_j \geq 0;$$

$$(j = 1, 2, \ldots\ldots N)\}$$

The set S is also known as the free disposal convex hull of the observed input-output bundles. One can obtain various measures of efficiency of a firm using the set S as the reference technology.

For a commercial firm, both inputs and outputs will be choice variables and the only constraint would be the feasibility of the input-output bundle chosen. For such a firm, criterion of efficiency is profit maximization. At input and output prices w and p, respectively, the actual profit of the firm producing the output bundle Y^o from the input bundle X^o is $\prod^o = p^/ Y^o - w^/ X^o$. The maximum profit feasible for the firm is:

$\prod(w, p) = \max p^/ Y - w^/ X : (X,Y) \in T.$

In any empirical application, the maximum profit may be obtained as

$\prod^* = \max p^/ Y - w^/ X$ s.t.

$$\sum_{j=1}^{N} \lambda_j X^j \geq Y; \sum_{j=1}^{N} \lambda_j X^j \leq X; \sum_{j=1}^{N} \lambda_j \geq 0; \; (j = 1, 2, \ldots\ldots N)\}$$

The profit efficiency of the firm is measured as $\delta = \prod^o/\prod^*$. This measure is also bounded between 0 and 1 except in case where the actual profit is negative, while the maximum profit is positive. In that case δ is less than 0. If the maximum profit is negative as well, δ exceeds unity (Das *et al.*, 2005).

2. The important findings of Economic Surveys by OECD (2007) on major Indian states are:

   i) With relatively more liberal states receiving virtually all of India's FDI flows (p.93).

   ii) Excessive administrative burden are associated with lower share of private sector employment in the formal sector: firms in the relatively restrictive states prefer to remain small and informal so as to avoid government administrative requirements (p.93).

   iii) States in which regulation of product is more conducive to competition have been far more successful at infrastructure provision than the relatively restrictive states (p.197-98).

References

Ahluwalia, Montek S. (2000). "Economic Performance of States in Post–Reform Period", *Economic and Political Weekly*, 6 May.

Banker, R.D., A. Charnes, and W.W. Coper (1984): 'Some Models for Estimating Technical and Scale Efficiencies in Data Envelopment Analysis', *Management Science* , 30(9)(September), pp. 1078–1092.

Bhattacharya, B.B. and S. Sakthivel (2004). "Regional Growth and Disparity in India: Comparison of Pre- and Post-Reform Decades", *Economic and Political Weekly*, 29(10), 6th March.

Charnes, A., W.W. Copper, and E. Rhodes (1978): 'Measuring the Efficiency of Decision Making Units', *European Journal of Operation Research* 2 (6), pp. 429–444.

Charnes, A., T.C. Charles, W.W. Cooper and B. Golany (1985): "A Development Study of Data Environment Analysis in Measuring the Efficiency of Maintenance Units in the U.S. Air Force, In: Russell, G. and Robert Thrall, G. (Eds.)", *Analysis of Operation Research*, 2(1), 95–111.

Das, A., A. Nag and S.C. Ray (2005): "Liberalisation, Ownership and Efficiency in Indian Banking: A Nonparametric Analysis", *Economic and Political Weekly*, May 19.

OECD (2007): "Organization for Economic Co-operation and Development Surveys: India", *Academic Foundations*, New Delhi.

OECD (2002): "Productivity and Innovation: The Impact of Product and Labour Market Policies", OECD Economic Outlook 71. Preliminary Edition: Paris.

Rao, H., "Growing Regional Disparities in Development in India", *Indian Economic Journal*, 54(1), April-June, 2006.

Crime, Deterrence and Growth in Post Liberalised India—An Application of Seemingly Unrelated Regression Equation Model

Mousumi Dutta and Zakir Husain*

1. Introduction

Crime degrades quality of life in many ways. It limits movement, thereby impeding access to possible employment and educational opportunities; it also discourages the accumulation of assets. As crime makes people risk averse, it discourages entrepreneurial and other economic activity. Crime is also more 'expensive' for poor people in poor countries, as it (particularly violent crimes) can lead to medical costs and loss of productivity that poor people in developing countries are ill equipped to bear (UN, 2005). From a macro perspective, crime undermines the ability of the state to promote development.[1] High crime rates can drive out foreign and domestic investment[2] as well as skilled or high productive labor. Further, activities like tourism (capable of generating substantial revenue), are especially sensitive to crime rates.

Controlling crime rates, therefore, is particularly important in developing countries like India. Although large sums are spent on establishing and maintaining the police force and judicial system in developing countries, such intervention will be effective only if they are based on an understanding of crime and the factors determining crime rates. Consequently research that identifies determinants of criminal behavior and explores the relationships existing between criminal activity and different socio economic variables has substantial policy relevance.

Initial theories of crime emphasized the effect of poverty and social deprivation on crime rates (Shaw and McKay, 1942, Clowrad and Ohlin, 1960, Merton, 1968). Economists began studying crime from the 1960s. In his pioneering study, Fleisher (1963, 1966) argued that crime rates are positively associated with unemployment and low income levels. Ehrlich (1973), too, showed that low income levels led to high crime rates.

---

*This paper is based on a project funded by Indian Council of Social Science Research.

Becker (1968), however, argued that a criminal should be viewed, not as a helpless victim of social oppression, but a rational economic agent. Like any other people, the potential criminal weighs costs/risks and benefits when deciding whether or not to commit crime: some individuals become criminals because of the financial and other rewards from crime compared to legal work, taking account of the likelihood of apprehension and conviction, and the severity of punishment (Becker, 1968: 176).

Among other important issues examined in the literature on crime were the effects of police presence, convictions, and the severity of punishment on the level of criminal activity (Becker, 1968, Ehrlich, 1973, 1975, 1996). This led to the development of deterrence theory, arguing that potential crimes evaluate both the risk of being caught and the associated punishment. The empirical evidence from developed countries confirm that both these factors have a negative effect on crime rates.

Following these theories, a substantial body of empirical literature has originated in developed countries, attempting to identify determinants of crime. Instances of such studies in developing countries, however, are rare. In fact this paper is possibly the first attempt to undertake a rigorous econometric analysis of determinants of crime in India. The objective of this paper is to examine the impact of deterrence and socio-economic variables on crime rates in Indian states after the economic liberalisation of the 1990s. In particular, we seek to verify whether the theories of crime originating in developed countries are relevant in developing countries.

The paper is arranged as follows. Section 2 presents some statistics on crime rates in India followed by a discussion of the methodology. We clarify the basis for selecting the variables used in the analysis and the nature of hypothesized relation of these variables with crime rates. This is followed by a justification of the econometric method. Section 3 presents the results, and extends the basic model by incorporating endogeneity. The paper concludes by discussing the implications of the findings.

2. Data Sources and Methodology

Crime in India

In India, the Criminal Procedure Code divides crimes into two heads: cognizable and non-cognizable. In the case of cognizable crimes, the police has the responsibility to take action on receipt of a complaint or of credible information. This action constitutes visiting the scene of crime, investigating the facts, apprehending the offender and producing the offending persons before the appropriate court of law. Cognizable crimes are again sub-divided as those falling under either the Indian Penal Code (IPC), or under the Special and Local Laws (SLL).[3] Non-cognizable crimes, on the other hand, are left to be pursued by the affected parties themselves in Courts. The police force initiates investigation into such crimes only with the permission of the magistrate. Following literature, this paper considers only IPC crimes. The reason is that the socio-economic factors are less important in determining SLL crimes. Further, they constitute a negligible fraction of reported crime.

In India statistics on crime are published annually by the National Crime Records Bureau, under the Ministry of Home Affairs. State-wise data is available on number of different crimes committed, enforcement mechanism and judicial institutions in a standardized format. An analysis of the trend in crime rate over the study period reveals an overall increasing trend, with a sharp decrease in 2003 (Fig. 9.1). The rate of increase, however, is modest – 9.2% between 1997 and 2006. This represents an annual increase of only 0.9%.

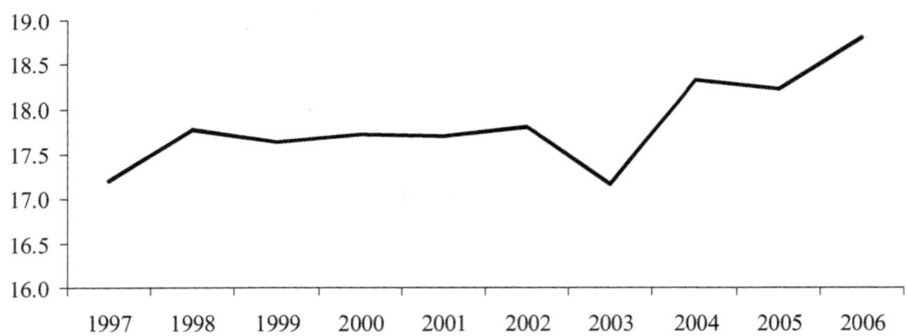

Fig. 9.1: Trends in IPC in India — 1999 to 2006

A comparison of the share of major types of crime committed in total IPC crimes in 1999 and 2006 (Fig. 9.2) shows marginal differences. Violent crimes and property related crimes remain the domiant form of criminal activity in both the years. The largest increase has been for crimes against body (murder, attempt to murder, culpable homicide, kidnapping and abduction, etc.). There has also been a slight increase in economic crimes (criminal breach of trust, cheating and counterfeiting) and crimes against women, while property-related crimes (dacoity, robbery, burglary, theft, etc.) and crimes against public order have fallen by about 2%.

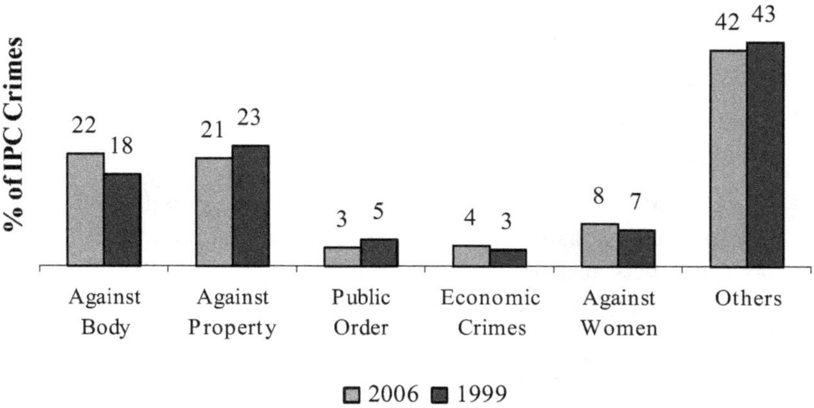

Fig. 9.2: Changes in Type of Crime– 1999 and 2006

Crime Function

The hypothesis of this paper is that crime rates depend upon the deterrence effect and on the socio-economic structure. These two variables may be further decomposed into the following variables:

1. **Deterrence Variables:** Deterrence variables like probabilities of being arrested and convicted determine the expected returns from crime (Becker, 1968, Ehrlich, 1973, 1975, 1996, Grogger, 1991). Since these probabilities represent costs to criminals, their expected signs are negative.

   Now, the probability of being arrested depends on police performance, which may be reflected by indicators like number of policemen per 1,000 of population, number of IPC cases per civil policeman (representing load on the police force), rate of arrest (per thousand population), charge sheets filed as percentage of cases in which investigations were completed (that is, probability of being charge-sheeted after committing a crime). On the other hand the probability of conviction depends on judiciary performance–conviction rates (proportion of cases tried resulting in convictions, representing the probability of being punished) and percentage of IPC cases disposed off within six months (speed in which punishment will occur). Data pertaining to these indicators are available in the annual publication by the National Crime Records Bureau.

2. **Socio-Economic Variables:** The following socio-economic variables have been included in the analysis:

(a) *Economic Growth*: Fleisher (1963, 1966) and Ehrlich (1973) argued the *level* of growth, an indicator of the level of economic prosperity, as an important determinant of crime rates. In this paper, State Domestic Product at factor cost (constant at 1993-94 prices) has been used as a measure of economic growth.

More important, however, is the quality of growth rather than quantity of growth (or growth rate). This is captured through poverty levels, urbanization and level of education.

(b) *Inequality*: Criminal activities are determined by economic motivations. Such motivations may be created by a sense of frustration, or an "envy effect" (Kelley, 2000). A higher income inequality also means a worsening of legitimate earning opportunity, hence there is a possibility that a rise in income inequality would increase crime – not only by creating potential criminals, but also potential victims having material goods worth seizing (Fleisher, 1966, Ehrlich, 1973, Chiu and Madden, 1998, Burdett *et al.*, 1999, Kelly, 2000, Fajnzylber *et al.*, 2002, Burdett and Mortensen, 1998, Juhn, *et al.*, 1993, Pratt and Godsey, 2003). Inequality levels are estimated from unit level National Sample Survey data.

(c) *Urbanization*: The structural transformation from a predominantly rural economy to an urban one may increase the crime rate through different channels. For instance, increased levels of migration from rural to urban areas may stimulate an increase in criminal activities (Fisher, 1987). Attempts of elite groups to modernize is another relevant facor (Fisher, 1987). Urbanisation leads to congestion and insanitary living conditions. This generates social tension and leads to eruptions of violence and crime, particularly in communities characterized by diversity (UN, 2005). Urbanization may also marginalize a section of the population, driving them out of the legal market economy and forcing them to adopt criminal activities for their livelihood. The rate of urbanization is also important (UN, 2005). Rapidly urbanizing areas may have more unstable population[4] and little sense of community. This may lead to erosion of traditional collective socio-religious norms controlling crime (UN 2005). Urbanization figures are available in the Union Primary Census Abstract, published by the Registrar General of Census Operations.

(d) *Education*: Higher levels of educational attainment raise skill and abilities and are associated with higher returns in the labor market, thereby increasing the opportunity cost of criminal behavior (Freeman, 1991, 1996, Grogger, 1995, 1998, Lochner and Moretti, 2001). Education may also have a 'civilization effect', by improving moral stance and promoting the virtues of hard work and honesty (Fajnzylber et. al., 2002, Usher, 1997).

This paper considers the proportion of people having at least middle class level of education in each state. This is available from the Census authorities.

The source of data for each variable is given in the Appendix.

Choice of Econometric Model

The hypothesized form of the crime rate function therefore takes the following form:

CRATE = ϕ(PM_D, IPC_PM, AR1, CSR1, CVR1, LPCSDP, URBAN, MEDU, INEQ) [1]

when,

CRATE	:	Number of IPC crimes per '00,000 population
PM_D	:	No. of police men per '000 square kilometer
IPC_PM	:	No. of IPC cases per civil policeman
AR1	:	Number of arrests in IPC cases per '00,000 population in previous period
CSR1	:	Percentage of IPC cases investigated in which charge sheets were filed in previous period
CVR1	:	Conviction rate in previous period
PCSDP	:	Log of Per capita SDP at factor cost (constant price 1993–94)
INEQ	:	Value of Gini coefficient for expenditure levels
URBAN	:	Urbanization level
MEDU	:	Percentage of persons with at least middle level of education

While most econometric analysis of crime rates assume that *current values* of deterrence variables affect the crime rate, this paper incorporates a *lagged adjustment process*. The reason is that potential offenders can observe the values of deterrence-related variables (AR,

CSR and CVR) realized in the *previous* period, and estimate the probability of being apprehended and punished in the current period based on these observations.

Panel data on major Indian states has been used in this paper. The data relates to the period 1999-2005. Econometric theory suggests that in such cases either of the following two forms may be used:

(i) *Fixed Effect Model*: In this case intercept terms are assumed to be independent of X_{it}. The regression equation in terms of a single explanatory variable can be presented as

$$CRATE_{it} = \alpha_i + \beta X_{it} + u_i \qquad [1a]$$

where α_i are intercept terms that vary across states (or state groups), but remain invariant across time. The OLS method is used to estimate [1a]. Recent works on crime, using panel data, adopt this method (Neumayer, 2003).

(ii) *Random Effect Model*: Alternately, the intercept terms may be correlated with the explanatory variables. In that case, α_i are modeled as random variables and treated at par with the error term.

$$CRATE_{it} = \beta X_{it} + e_i \qquad [1b]$$

where $e_i = \alpha_i + u_i$. Since the error terms of same cross-sectional units become correlated—though errors from different cross-sectional units remain independent[5]—Generalized Least Square (GLS), rather than OLS, should be used to estimate the model.

We argue that neither of these approaches is suitable in the present case. The situation in states like Kerala and Andhra Pradesh (where substantial progress has been made in human development) vary from under-developed states like Bihar, Madhya Pradesh, Rajasthan and Uttar Pradesh, or states like Maharashtra and Gujarat (where the level of industrialization is high, but this has failed to reduce poverty levels). Therefore the regression model no longer remains a single equation, but is transformed into *a set of stacked equations* (Green, 2002: 615) that can be represented as follows:

$$\begin{bmatrix} y_1 \\ y_2 \\ . \\ . \\ y_m \end{bmatrix} = \begin{bmatrix} X_1 & 0 & . & . & 0 \\ 0 & X_2 & . & . & 0 \\ . & 0 & . & . & . \\ . & . & . & . & . \\ 0 & 0 & . & . & X_m \end{bmatrix} \begin{bmatrix} \beta_1 \\ \beta_2 \\ . \\ . \\ \beta_m \end{bmatrix} + \begin{bmatrix} u_1 \\ u_2 \\ . \\ . \\ u_m \end{bmatrix} \qquad [1c]$$

where y_i, β_i and u_i are vectors and X_i, are matrices for each state group ($i = 1, 2, \ldots m$).

Apparently the individual classical regression equations in [1c] are unrelated. Zellner (1962), however, points out that even these seemingly unrelated regression equations (SURE) may be linked statistically, though not structurally. Such links may be established through subtle interactions if "the response of the dependent variable to an explanatory variable is different for different individuals but for a given individual it is constant over time" (Judge et al, 1985: 539). This will result in random disturbances associated with at least some of the different equations being correlated with each other in a specific way—the disturbances will be independent over time, but correlated across cross-section units. The joint nature of distribution of error terms and non-diagonal nature of the associated variance-covariance matrix will arise if there are omitted variables that are common to all equations. For instance, factors like the presence of a common civil code and procedure, spill-over effects of socio-economic developments in states, macro-economic changes in the Indian economy, and so on, may be the omitted factors subtly linking the equations for states in the present case.

In this situation, estimation of parameters by OLS—which treats the model as a set of distinct equations—may generate consistent, but not efficient, estimators:

> ... treating the model as a collection of separate relationships will be sub-optimal when drawing inferences about the model's parameters. Indeed, ... in general the sharpness of these inferences may be improved by taking account of the jointness inherent in the SURE model rather than ignoring it. (Srivastava and Giles, 1986: 2).

In such cases, Zellner (1962) advocates the application of GLS to the stacked model to ensure asymptotic efficiency of the estimators. Application of this method is not common in the literature on crime – Pogue's analysis (1986) seems to be the only application of the SURE model.

3. Results and Discussion

Basic Model

The result for model [1] is given in Table 9.1. The values of chi-square and the pseudo-R^2 are both high.

Table 9.1: Seemingly Unrelated Regression

Equation	*Obs*	*Parms*	*RMSE*	*"R-sq"*	*chi2*	*P*
crate	153	9	40.17941	0.6651	303.91	0.0000

Crate	*Coef.*	*Std. Err.*	*z*	*p>|z|*	*[95% conf.*	*Interval]*
lpcsdp	55.10487	12.0677	4.57	0.000	31.45262	78.75712
urban	–.1161838	.3696654	–0.31	0.753	–.8407146	.608347
medu	.6106737	.4497421	1.36	0.175	–.2708046	1.492152
ineq	–178.7391	90.52834	–1.97	0.048	–356.1713	–1.306771
pm_d	–.217824	.1092243	–1.99	0.046	–.4318997	–.0037483
ipc_pm	33.15474	3.98676	8.32	0.000	25.34084	40.96865
ar1	11.36068	2.28241	4.98	0.000	6.887236	15.83412
csr1	.7262945	.2492461	2.91	0.004	.2377811	1.214808
cvr1	.699804	.1865921	3.75	0.000	.3340902	1.065518
_cons	–215.9449	48.72119	–4.43	0.000	–311.4366	–120.4531

It can be seen that the coefficients LPCSDP and all the deterrence variables are statistically significant. Analysis of the correlation matrix for the socio-economic variables shows that LPCSDP is highly correlated with URBAN and MEDU; further, these two variables are also strongly correlated with each other. This would imply the presence of multi-collinearity and explain the relatively low t-values observed for these two variables. The correlation between INEQ and LPCSDP, on the other hand, is not very high (0.2366).

Table 9.2: Correlation Matrix of Socio-Economic Variables

	lpcsdp	*medu*	*urban*	*ineq*
Lpcsdp	1.0000			
Medu	0.5260	1.0000		
Urban	0.5497	0.4619	1.0000	
Ineq	0.2366	0.0124	0.1512	1.0000

Analysis of the sign of coefficients of socio-economic variables reveals an interesting picture. Economic growth has actually led to an increase in crime rates. The reason lies in the nature of the growth process occurring after liberalization:

1. Liberalization has increased inequalities, and hence social tension.
2. The capital intensive nature of industrialization has squeezed the growth of employment opportunities for the general public.
3. Rising consumerism has led to a sharp increase in consumer demand. Coupled with restrictions on legal means to satisfy this demand, this may lead to an increase tendency towards relying on criminal means to satisfy this demand.

Simultaneously, rising education levels – without any corresponding increase in economic opportunities for the masses – seems to have increased frustration with legal means of livelihood, thereby leading to higher levels of crime. The increasing employment opportunities created by urbanization, predictably, has lowered crime rates. Although INEQ has a negative coefficient, it is not statistically significant.

The coefficients of deterrence variables, except PM_D, are all positive. While the signs of IPC_PM and PM_D are expected – increasing pressure on the police force or fewer policemen will both encourage a potential criminal to think that (s)he can get away with crime – the positive values of variables like AR1, CSR1 and CVR1 do not match with empirical findings in developed countries.

Introducing Endogeneity

One possible reason for the unexpected signs of some of the coefficients may be the presence of endogeneity in the model—the deterrence variables both determine and are determined by crime rates (Ehrlich, 1973, 1975, Brier and Fienberg, 1980, Pogue, 1986). For instance, arrest rates is determined by lagged crime rates, while increasing arrest following complaints before the police may lead to higher number of charge sheets. This implies that model [1] should be revised to:

$$\text{CRATE} = \phi\,(\text{PM\_D, IPC\_PM, AR1, CSR1, CVR1, LPCSDP, URBAN, MEDU, INEQ}) \quad [2a]$$

$$\text{AR1} = \eta\,(\text{CRATE2}) \quad [2b]$$

$$\text{CSR1} = \gamma\,(\text{AR1}) \quad [2c]$$

where CRATE2: Two period lagged crime rate

The system of simultaneous equations given by [2a] to [2c] has also been estimated using Zellner's SURE model.

Table 9.3: Seemingly Unrelated Regression with Endogeneity

Equation	*Obs*	*Parms*	*RMSE*	*"R-sq"*	*chi2*	*P*
crate	126	9	21.15155	0.9080	1514.31	0.0000
ar1	126	1	.4128065	0.8568	826.26	0.0000
csr1	126	1	13.63342	0.4295	79.97	0.0000

	Coef.	*Std. Err*	*z*	*P > |z|*	*[95% Conf. Interval]*	
Crate						
lpcsdp	28.69313	6.036627	4.75	0.000	16.86156	40.5247
urban	–.2032224	.1711119	–1.19	0.235	–.5385955	.1321507
medu	–.2882367	.2163142	–1.33	0.183	–.7122047	.1357313
ineq	–50.53942	45.70085	–1.11	0.269	–140.1114	39.03261
pm_d	–.0241665	.0522156	–0.46	0.643	–.1265072	.0781741
ipc_pm	6.315295	2.410503	2.62	0.009	1.590796	11.03979
ar1	64.24988	2.719007	23.63	0.000	58.92073	69.57904
csr1	–.5768609	.1331665	–4.33	0.000	–.8378624	–.3158593
cvr1	.3429576	.0895689	3.83	0.000	.1674059	.5185094
_cons	–68.1377	25.11722	–2.71	0.007	–117.3665	–18.90886
ar1						
crate2	.0148316	.000516	28.74	0.000	.0138203	.0158428
_cons	–.1436531	.0916594	–1.57	0.117	–.3233022	.0359959
csr1						
ar1	9.865635	1.103216	8.94	0.000	7.703371	12.0279
_cons	49.01142	2.78197	17.62	0.000	43.55886	54.46398

Crime rates, is again found to be positively related to lagged arrest and conviction rates. One reason for this may be that the corruption and malpractices prevailing in most Indian jails makes it difficult for prisoners to discard their criminal tendencies. In fact, conviction often brutalizes persons imprisoned for simple felonies (Piehl and DiIulio, 1995). Further, arrest and convictions typically mark a person as a permanent deviant, reducing his access to legal channels of livelihood (Grogger, 1995, Holzer *et al.*, 2003, Pager, 2003, Seiter and Kadela, 2003). In other words, arrest or conviction may perversely reinforce criminal behavior in many cases, so that criminals get caught in a 'crime trap'.[6] Data from the National Crime Records Bureau reveal that recidivism is quite high—nearly 10 per cent of arrested persons had previous criminal records.

Expectedly, the presence of more police personnel per square kilometer[7] and fewer IPC cases per policemen are both associated with lower crime rates. High rates of charge sheeting, too, act as a deterrent, to reduce crime rates.

Among the socio-economic variables, INEQ continues to remain insignificant. Among the other variables, economic growth has a positive effect on crime rates, while urbanization and education are negatively related with crime rates.

4. Conclusion

Our empirical exercise shows that the theory of criminal behaviour originating in the developed countries has limited relevance for developing economies like India. Given the demographic pressure and nature of economic growth in developing countries, the channels through which socio-economic variables and deterrence factors operate in developed countries get blocked or even distorted. This leads to causal relationships that do not match with empirical findings for developed countries, implying the need to take into account the specific causal mechanism operating in India while designing crime control measures.

In India, for instance, intervention to control and reduce crime rate has relied on increasing expenditure on the police and judicial systems. This is expected to act as a deterrent by increasing the expected costs of committing a crime – as the probability of getting detected and punished will increase. This is in line with empirical findings for developed countries, showing that deterrence is likely to have a significant negative impact on crime rates.

However, the results of this econometric analysis show that high conviction rates will actually increase crime rates. This reveals inherent flaws in the criminal detection and corrective system. There is need for reforming the penal system to enable this system to rectify the behavioral pattern of criminals through education and the imparting of technical and vocational training, so that they may return to the mainstream after their release.

Results of this paper show that economic growth and, in particular, its quality, is an important determinant of crime rates. Liberalization of the Indian economy has led to an acceleration of growth; the results of the endogenous model show that this need not reduce crime. This implies that growth process has to be participatory and create opportunities for the entire population in order to control crime rates.

Notes

1. A study of Brazil estimates that a 10 percent reduction in the homicide rate may raise per capita income by 0.2-0.8 percent over the next five years (World Bank, 2006).
2. As investors may view crime as sign of social instability, and feel that crime drives up the cost of doing business. Such costs include loss of goods, hiring security guards, building fences, installing alarm systems or security devices, and so on.
3. SLL includes Arms Act, Gambling Act, Excise Act, Indian Passport Act, Copyright Act and so on. See page 27 of Crime in India, 2002 for a complete list.
4. Rate at which population changes households is high (UN, 2005).
5. That is $cov(e_{it}, e_{is}) \neq 0$, though $cov(e_{it}, e_{jt})$.
6. Piehls and DiIulio (1995) cites an estimate of Lawrence Greenfeld (US Bureau of Justice Statistics) that 94% of all State prisoners have either been convicted of a violent crime or been previously sentenced to probation or incarceration. Another study reports that two out of every three parolees re-enter prisons (Little Hoover Commission, 2003). Murray (2007) argues that even children of convicted parents may be socially excluded. This may lead to development of criminal tendencies amongst them later on.
7. Although the coefficient of PM_D is not significant, it appears to be correlated with PM_POP (-0.3308).

References

Arthur, J.A. (1991): "Socio-economic predictors of crime in rural Georgia". *Criminal Justice Review*, 16: 29–41.

Becker, G.S., (1968): "Crime and Punishment: An Economic Approach", *Journal of Political Economy*, 76 (2): 169–217.

Becker, G.S., (1993): "Nobel Lecture: The Economic Way at Looking at Behavior". *Journal of Political Economy*, 101(3): 385–409.

Bennet, R.R. (1991): "Development and crime: A cross-national, time-series analysis of competing models". *The Sociological Quarterly*, 32(3): 343–363.

Box, (1987): *Recession, crime and punishment* (Totowa: Barnes & Noble).

Braithwaite, J. and V. Braithwaite (1980): "The effect of income inequality and social democracy on homicide." *British Journal of Criminology*, 21: 421–438.

Brier, S.S. and S.E. Fienberg (1980): "Recent Econometric Modelling of Crime and Punishment: Suport for the Deterrence Hypothesis?" *Evaluation Review*, 4(2): 147–191.

Cloward, R. and Lloyd Ohlin (1960): *Delinquency and Opportunity*. (New York: The Free Press).

Crutchfield, R.D. (1989): "Labor stratification and violent crime." *Social Forces*, 68(2): 489–512.

Dersham, H.A. (1990): "Community Crime Prevention: A Review Essay on Program Evaluations and Policy Implications". *Criminal Justice Policy Review*, 90(1): 53–68.

Ehrlich, I., (1973): "Participation in Illegitimate Activities: A Theoretical and Empirical Investigation". *Journal of Political Economy*, 81(3): 521–565.

Ehrlich, I., (1975): "On the Relation between Education and Crime", in Juster, F.T. (ed.): *Education, Income and Human Behavior*. McGraw-Hill, New York: 313–337.

Ehrlich, I., (1996): "Crime, Punishment, and the Market for Offenses". *Journal of Economic Perspectives*, 10(1): 43–67.

Ehrlich, I., (1981): "On the Usefulness of Controlling Individuals: An Economic Analysis of Rehabilitation, Incapacitation and Deterrence". *American Economic Review*, 71 (3): 307–322.

Ehrlich, I. and G.D. Brower (1987): "On the Issue of Causality in the Economic Model of Crime and Law Enforcement: Some Theoretical Considerations and Experimental Evidence". *American Economic Review*, 77 (2): 99–106.

Fajnzylber, P., Lederman, D. and N. Loayza (2002): "What Causes Violent Crime?" *European Economic Review*, 46 (2): 1323–1357.

Fisher, S. (1987): "Economic Development and Crime: The two may be associated as an adaptation to industrialism in Social Revolution." *American Journal of Economics and Sociology*, 46(1): 17–34.

Fleisher, B., (1963): "The Effect of Unemployment on Juvenile Delinquency". *Journal of Political Economy*, 71(6): 543–555

Fleisher, B., (1966): "The Effects of Income on Delinquency", *American Economic Review*, 56 (1/2): 118–137

Freeman, R.B., (1991): "Crime and the Employment of Disadvantaged Youths", NBER Working Paper no. 3875.

Freeman, R.B., (1996): "Why Do So Many Young American Men Commit Crimes and What Might We Do About It?" *Journal of Economic Perspectives*, 10(1): 25–42.

Gelsthorpe, L. and Morris, A. (2002): "Women"s imprisonment in England and Wales: A penal paradox". *Criminology and Criminal Justice*, 2(3): 277–301.

Greene, W.J. (2002): *Econometric Analysis*, (New Delhi: Pearson Education Institution).

Grogger, J., (1991): "Certainty vs. Severity of Punishment". *Economic Inquiry*, 29: 297–309.

Grogger, J., (1995): "The Effect of Arrest on the Employment and Earnings of Young Men". *Quarterly Journal of Economics*, 110(1): 51–72.

Grogger, J., (1998): "Market Wages and Youth Crime". *Journal of Labor Economics*, 16: 756–91.

Holzer, H., Raphael, S., and Stoll, M. (2003): "Employer demand for ex-offenders: Recent evidence from Los Angeles", Paper presented at the Urban Institute Roundtable on Offender Re-Entry, New York, March.

Hsieh, C.C. and M.D. Pugh (1993): "Poverty, Income Inequality and Violent Crime: A Meta-analysis of Recent Aggregate Studies." *Criminal Justice Review*, 18(2): 182–202

Judge, G., Hill, C., Griffiths, W. and Lee, T. (1985): *The Theory and Practice of Econometrics,* (New York: John Wiley & Sons).

Little Hoover Commission. (2003): "Back to the community: Safe and sound parole policies", Sacramento, CA. Available at *www.lhc. ca.gov/lhcdir/172/report172. pdf*, accessed on 4 September 2008.

Lochner, L. and E. Moretti (2001): "The effect of education on crime: evidence from prison inmates, arrests, and self-reports", *NBER Working Paper* no. 8605.

Mehlum, H., K. Moene and R. Torvik (2005): "Crime induced poverty traps." *Journal of Development Economics*, 77(2): 325–340.

Merton, R. (1968): *Social Theory and Social Structure*. 2nd Rev. ed. (New York: The Free Press).

Messner, S.F. (1983): "Regional differences in the economic correlates of the urban homicide rate: Some evidence on the importance of cultural context." *Criminology*, 21: 477–488.

Murray, J. (2007): "The cycle of punishment: Social exclusion of prisoners and their children". *Criminology and Criminal Justice*, 7(1): 55–81.

National Crime Records Bureau (2003): *Crime in India*, (New Delhi: Govt. of India).

Needels, K.E. (1996): "Go directly to jail and do not collect? A long term study of recidivism, employment and earnings pattern among prison releasees." *Journal of Research in Crime and Delinquency*, 33(4): 471–496.

Neumayer, E. (2003): "Good Policy Can Lower Violent Crime: Evidence from a cross-National Panel of Homicide Rates, 1980–97", *Journal of Peace Research,* 40(6): 619–640.

Pager, D. (2003): "The mark of a criminal record". *American Journal of Sociology*, 108, 937–975.

Piehls, A.M. and J.J. DiIulio, Jr. (1995): ""Does Crime Pay?" Revisited". *Brookings Review Magazine*, Winter: 21–25.

Pogue, T.F. (1986): "Offender Expectations and Identification of Crime Supply Functions". *Evaluation Review*, 10(4): 455–482

Seiter, R.P. and Kadela, K.P. (2003): "Prisoner reentry: What works, what does not, and what is promising". *Crime & Delinquency*, 49(3): 360–388.

Shaw, Clifford R. and McKay, Henry D. (1942): "*Juvenile Delinquency and Urban Areas,* (Chiago: The University of Chicago Press).

Sutherland, E.H. (1949): "*White Collar Crimes"*, (New York: Dryden Press).

United Nations (2005): *Crime and Development in Africa,* (New York: United Nations).

Usher, D., (1997): "Education as Deterrent to Crime". *Canadian Journal of Economics*, 30(2): 367–84.

World Bank (2007): *Crime, Violence and Economic Development in Brazil: Elements for Effective Public Policy*, (Washington: World Bank).

Zellner, A. (1962): "Efficient Method of Estimating Seemingly Unrelated Regressions and Tests of Aggregation Bias." *Journal of American Statistical Association*, 57: 500–509.

The Impact of Inefficient Institution on Health in India

Ankita Mitra, Ismeet Sondhi, Shilpi Mukherjee and Debnarayan Sarker

What are the main obstacles for healthcare services of public sector in India? There are some vital issues adversely affecting health care services of public sector in India. These are: absenteeism from place of work, lack of policies for human resource development, poor payment systems and dual practice. As regards the first issue is concerned, a majority of doctors opt for specialization and/or urban practice. The reluctance to serve in rural areas has become a major impediment in the government's ability to provide health services to the rural population. Not surprisingly, absenteeism among doctors and front-line workers from their place of work is high. A study conducted by the World Bank (2004) and other studies show absenteeism ranging from 40-45% among doctors working in primary health centres. The World Bank Study based on a simple regression analysis showed the relationship between income and absenteeism, which suggested that higher income states have lower rate of absenteeism with point value at 0.001, meaning that every increase of □ 1000 State per capita income is associated with a reduction in absence of 1% point, with p values on the co-efficient on income at 0.13. However, this is a crude analysis as, at another level, absenteeism is high in those rich States where doctors are also engaged in private practice. Punjab has the lowest utilization of public facilities only because of large-scale absenteeism of doctors. The second issue is that the recruitment policy is a contributory factor for the lack of motivation among doctors to provide services in rural areas. The absence of transparent transfer policies, norms for deployment of personnel and reward for merit are some of the factors contributing to the deviant behavior among providers. Concerning the third issue, it is said that the increment in salary in the public sector is not based on performance—but in private sector we get performance linked package. There they value your performance. The private sector gets better results from the doctors when they offer them better packages. But the provision for performance linked packages is hardly observed in public sector. Therefore, in public sector we cannot get very high motivation by service providers. In private sector, they look at quantitative and qualitative performance appraisal. So, service providers in public sector usually do not work with passion. Finally, to compensate for the relatively low salaries, doctors are permitted private practice outside office hours or are given a non-practicing allowance, often 25% of the basic pay. Lack of monitoring, effective supervision and, at times, collusive relationships affects patient care in public facilities.

How are private and public sector working in the health care market in India? Today there are approximately 11,25,000 practitioners of different systems registered with various medical councils in the country. Of them, only 125,000 are in government service (including those in central health services, the armed forces, railways, state insurance etc). That leaves about a million doctors floating around in the private sector, not to mention tens of thousands of additional unqualified and unregistered medical practitioners. 59% of all practitioners are concentrated in cities. For instance, 60% of all medical graduates in Maharashtra are located in Mumbai, where no more than 11% of the state's population lives in. Similarly, 84% of hospital beds are today located in urban areas, whereas 75% of the population still resides in villages. This selective concentration of health care providers is a major concern to be addressed. The State offers subsidies, loans, tax waivers and other benefits for the setting up of private practice, hospitals, diagnostic centers and pharmaceuticals. Assuming that the government spends about □ 10 lakhs at current prices on the education and training of each doctor and about 80% of the out-turn of public medical schools either joins the private sector or migrates abroad, the country loses large resources which could have been used for public benefit. The country loses □ 4,000–5,000 million as a result of the out-migration of four to five thousand doctors every year. Thus, with such support the private health sector has grown into a giant – it is the largest private health sector in the world. With 60–80% of health care sought in the private sector, and households contributing 4–6% of their income, there's a whopping □ 400–600 billion health care market in India. It's mammoth size; notwithstanding, this sector has remained completely unregulated.

All over the world there is a tendency to move towards more organized national health system and an increased share of public finance in health care. Almost all developed capitalist and socialist countries have universal health care system where the public sector's share of the fiscal burden is between 60 to 100%. This trend is inevitable in the pursuit of equity and universal coverage.

How are the poor adversely affected by government doctors? Private practice by government doctors are another area of concern. Government salaried doctors practice in their private clinics when their duty is over, or also by minimizing their expected duty hours. Same physician may bear the role of both private and public service providers. In West Bengal, government doctors can practice in private settings after their duty is over. There exists good understanding between private and public doctors in terms of referrals to either side for their vested interests. Some health system research shows that patient party has to pay informally to government staffs in the few public settings. The impact of such system on the part of poor people is significant reduction in the access to care.

In this perspective the objective of this paper is to examine the effort level by the medical care providers between public medical services and private medical services. The underlying hypothesis is that both non-MBBS and MBBS exert much less effort in public medical services in relation to their efforts in private ones for the patients in different income areas (poor, middle and rich).

The Data Set

The data used for this study is mostly secondary in nature. We reviewed published articles from different sources such as articles from indexed journals through internet. The main source of data relates to the data of Institute of Socio-Economic Research on Democracy and Development (ISERDD, 2001). ISERDD (2001) began a longitudinal study of households in seven neighborhoods of Delhi. Three of the neighborhoods were poor, two middle income and two relatively wealthy. Over two years, 300 households were interviewed once a week for 35 weeks and once a month for another 8 months. Information was collected on health and health-care seeking behavior and demographic, income and consumption modules were administered twice in the two years. Less than 4 per cent of the households approached refused to participate. The demographic, educational and expenditure profiles of the households in the study are very similar to representative samples of Delhi residents in the National Sample Survey and the National Family Health Survey (Das and Sánchez 2004). Providers with a sign advertising medical care within a 15-minute walking radius around the periphery of the area of the household survey were also noted and interviewed. The procedure of measuring effort level appears in Table 10.1.

Table 10.1: What does Effort Measure

Sample	*Effort Categories or Country*	*The Effort Measure*	*Time Spent*	*Questions Asked of Patient*	*% who do Physical Exams*	*Poly-pharmacy (Total Number of Medicines Given)*
Delhi	Doctors who exert low effort	–1.1	1.9	1.36	14	2.13
	Doctors who exert medium effort	–0.3	3.36	2.94	78	2.72
	Doctors who exert high effort	1.13	6.15	5.32	98	3.05
	All Doctors	0.00	3.80	3.20	63	2.63

Results

How far does the disparity of effort appear between public doctors and their private counterparts in medical care received by patients? Figure 10.1, presenting the kernel density estimate for public and private providers of effort-in-practice (EIP) based on 4108 observations of doctor-patient interactions, shows that public doctors exert much less effort and less competence than their private counterparts. Differences in case-mix and severity might account for lower effort in the public sector. Less time with a patient is certainly reasonable if conditions seen in public clinics are much easier to treat and/or less severe than in private clinics. But the reality seems to be the opposite. The case mix in public and private venues are almost identical. Further, patients in public clinics are likely to be sicker than those in private, at least as measured by the number of days that symptoms had persisted before the patient sought help – a median of 5 days for private and 7 for public.

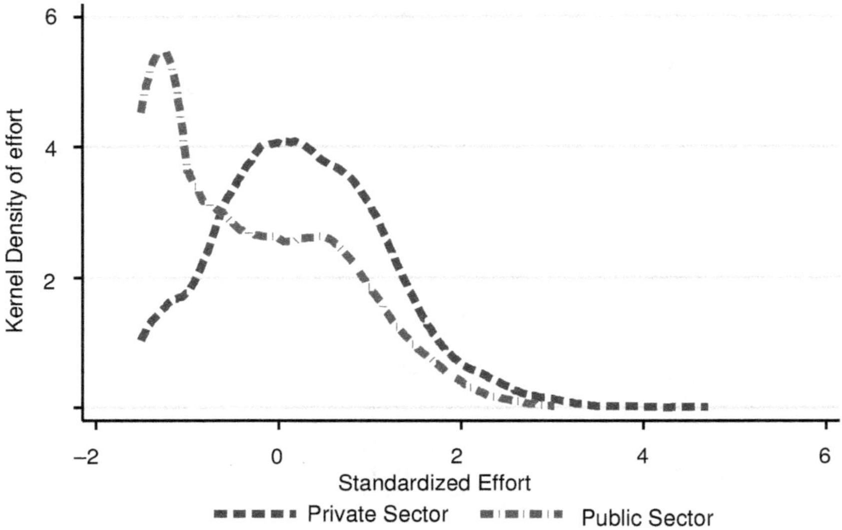

Fig. 10.1: Effort, Competence and Incentive

Notes: This shows a smoothed frequency distribution of effort across the public and the private sector based on 4,108 observations of doctor-patient interactions. Effort-in-practice or EIP is the principal components score based on the time spent with the patient, the number of history questions asked, the examinations performed and two questions related to information given.

Source: Money for Nothing—The Dire Straits of Medical Practice in Delhi, India; Jishnu Das and Jeffrey Hammer, The World Bank.

How far does the disparity of effort appear in real physical visit for the patients (for cough and diarrhea) between different types of public and private doctors? Figure 10.2 uses the subset of visits (and providers) in which the patient presented with either diarrhea or cough so that we have both the vignette from the practitioner and his/her actual practice for the very same condition. The graph compares the proportion of critical questions asked/examinations performed in the vignettes to the proportion asked in clinical observation for these two conditions. Several results are notable. First, while the non-MBBS providers knew fewer of the salient questions to ask/examinations to perform than either public or private MBBS doctors, they actually did approximately all they knew. Their practice and their competence are closely aligned. For MBBS doctors, however, the gap between what they know and what they do is large. Private practitioners completed only 59% of the tasks (questions/ examinations) that they knew to be important. Public sector doctors did less than a third of what they knew to be important. In fact, the non-MBBS providers ended up providing better care on average, by asking more of the salient questions and performing more of the critical examinations than the public MBBS doctors. Also important to note that the average real visit to an MBBS doctor took two minutes in the public and four minutes in the private sectors (inclusive of real physical examinations). However, the significant fact is that both non-MBBS and MBBS exert much less effort in public medical services in relation to their efforts in private ones.

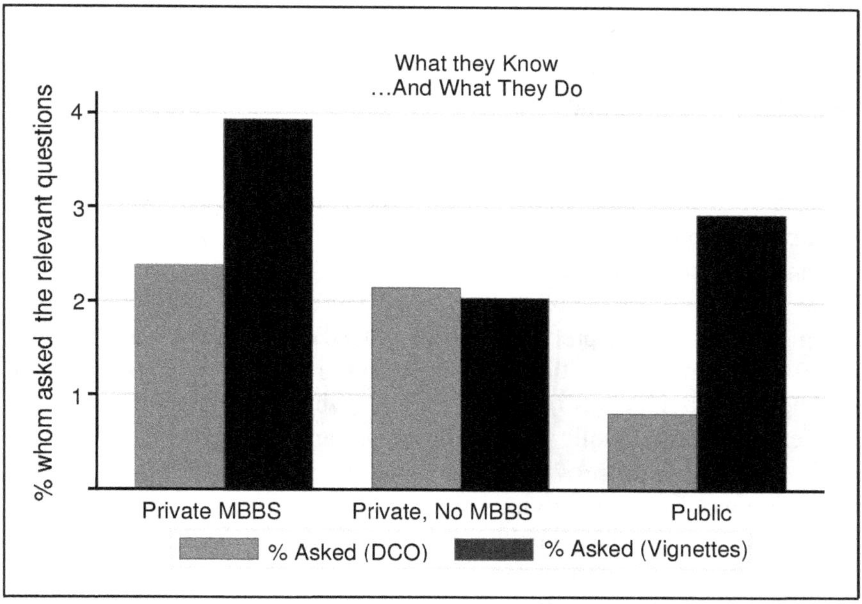

Fig. 10.2: Disparity of Efforts in Real Physical Visit

Notes: The figure compares questions asked in practice to those asked in the vignettes for patients reporting with diarrhea or cough without fever. The comparison is presented separately by the sector the doctor practices in and whether she holds an MBBS degree. The sample is restricted to those doctors who either saw a case of diarrhea or cough without fever during the observation. For cases of diarrhea, questions were (a) Has the patient had any vomiting; (b) The nature of the stool and (c) whether the patient had a temperature. For cough with fever, the questions were (a) experience of chest-pain; (b) the nature of the expectorant and (c) the history of fever. In addition, for both cases it was checked whether the doctor took the temperature of the patient, and for the cough case whether the doctor checked the blood-pressure of the patient. These two cases and the 9 specific tasks were covered in the vignettes previously.

Is there any change in the disparity of effort level for real physical visit, for the patients between different types of public and private doctors due to any reason, not simply those for cough and diarrhea? It appears in Figure 10.3. Here, for the full sample of doctors for which there is both a competence score and the effort-in-practice index (from visits for any reason, not simply those for cough and diarrhea) it appears the non-parametric regression line relating effort to competence. Providers in the private sector are separated by whether they had an MBBS degree or not and, public doctors, by whether they practice in a hospital or a clinic. Highly knowledgeable doctors may need less time to reach a diagnosis than less competent providers. In that case knowledge and effort would be substitutes and the function would be decreasing. The figure clearly shows that knowledge and effort are complementary since the functions are all increasing, and at similar rates for every level of competence. A second feature is that private doctors with an MBBS degree and public physicians in general hospitals look very similar. It is possible that the private sector puts in a little bit more effort at lower levels of competence but since the curves coincide at the high end, they are indistinguishable for at least some range of competence. Third, the private non-MBBS group lines up almost precisely with the MBBS providers. That is, as a function of competence, the degree of effort is unrelated to the type of training the provider has received. Finally, what really stands out is the difference between public doctors in clinics and dispensaries relative to every other type of provider. The amount of time, questions asked, examinations done and advice given are very much lower for public MBBS doctors in primary health clinics than anyone else. This leads us to suspect that the incentive structure–identical for all private providers–is more powerful as an explanation of the effort that providers exert than the qualification (whether MBBS or not) of the provider. The descriptive figures suggest some basic facts, some a little surprising, most fairly consistent with common knowledge. Medical care providers typically do less than what they know, more so for the public than the private sector. Public doctors in primary clinics in particular put in very little effort relative to their private counterparts. Finally, competence and effort appear to be complements and at rates that do not seem to vary much across the institutional affiliation or qualification of the provider. Despite the fact that the patterns observed in the raw-data, it needs to be cautious in interpreting these correlations. However, the vital issue that appears in Figure 10.3 are in conformity with that in Figure 10.2.

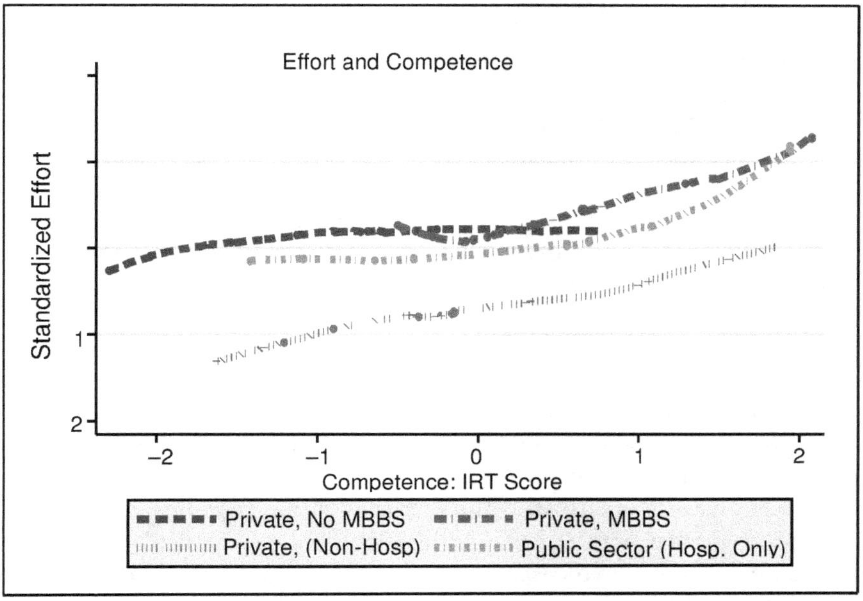

Fig. 10.3: Effort, Competence and Institutional Affiliations Revisited

Notes: The figure plots the (non-parametric) relationship between effort-in-practice and competence for practitioners in the private and public sector and practitioners with and without an MBBS degree (the rough equivalent of an MD in the US). Effort-in-practice or EIP is the principal components score based on the time spent with the patient, the number of history questions asked, the examinations performed and two questions related to information given. Competence refers to the Item Response score obtained in the vignettes administered previously (Das and Hammer 2005).

Source: Money for Nothing—The Dire Straits of Medical Practice in Delhi, India; Jishnu Das and Jeffrey Hammer, The World Bank.

The basic description illustrated in the Figures 10.1, 10.2 and 10.3 remains once we account for practitioner and patient characteristics (Tables 10.2 and 10.3). Table 10.2 shows that MBBS exert much less effort in public medical services in relation to their private ones, and difference between these two services is significant. Table 10.3 shows that effort increases with competence so that the complementarities of effort and competence along with positive valuation of cure is confirmed, both for the 9 tasks that were graded on the vignettes and in observation (Panel A) and the more general measure of effort (Panel B). Effort is lower in the public sector after accounting for differential workloads, patient populations and observed provider characteristics. Finally, public hospitals and other public health-care centers continue to differ, with the former performing significantly better. Whether hospitals are better or worse than the private sector depends on the dependent variable. For the 9 tasks (Panel A), the performance of hospitals is significantly worse than the private sector–F-tests of significance rejects equal performance at 1 percent levels of significance. For the overall measure of effort, there is no difference between hospitals and the private sector, with F-tests accepting the null at 10 percent confidence levels. Finally, 2.6 medicines are prescribed on average per encounter; the private sector prescribes between 20 and 25 per cent more medicines than public clinics and hospitals. All results are significant at the 1 percent level. Comparing the questions asked in clinical observation to those asked in the vignettes, the preferred specification suggests that the impact of competence on effort is small (Table 10.3, Panel A, Column 5). Increasing the probability of performing a task (either a question or an examination) in the vignettes from0 to 1 increases the probability of the task actually being performed in practice by at most 19 percentage points (estimates vary from 0.16 to 0.19). This increase is offset if the doctor is in the (non-hospital) public sector. Put another way, the probability that doctors will perform critical procedures for these two cases increases by 4 per cent when competence increases by 1 standard deviation; the difference between the public and the private sector is almost 4 times as high. The pattern is similar for the overall effort index (Panel B). An increase of one standard deviation incompetence leads to an increase of 0.21 standard deviations in the effort index. Practitioners in the (non-hospital) public sector report that effort levels are almost 0.8 standard deviations lower than their private counterparts. A difference of one standard deviation in competence corresponds closely to the difference between practitioners with and without MBBS degrees (Das and Hammer 2005). The adverse effects of the public sector on effort are almost 4 times as high as the beneficial effects of training. These estimates are robust to a number of controls. Aside from the workload of the practitioner, additional practitioner (qualification, age, experience and gender) and patient (age, gender and symptoms) characteristics have almost no impact on either the estimated coefficient of competence on effort or the estimated difference between the private and public sectors (Columns 1 to 4, Table 10.3, Panels A and B). In most specifications these additional characteristics are insignificant or mildly significant (not reported). However Figure 10.1 shows that public doctors exert much less effort and less competence than their private counterparts. In figures 10.2 and 10.3 it is observed that both non-MBBS and MBBS exert much less effort in public medical services in relation to their private ones for all types of visit to the patients. In conformity with all those issues that appear in Figures 10.1, 10.2 and

10.3, Table 10.3 also suggests that effort is determined primarily by incentives and competence, which act almost like sufficient statistics for the broader set of provider-level characteristics.

Table 10.2: Public and the Private Sector

Category	*Characteristics*	*Private*	*Public*	*Both Sectors*	*Difference Significant?*[a]
Doctor Characteristics	Age	44.48 (11.31)	43.76 (8.04)	44.32 (10.65)	NS
	Tenure in this location	13.69 (9.16)	9.88 (9.00)	12.85 (9.00)	<.05
	% Male	83% (37)	0.62 (0.49)	79% (41%)	<.01
	Average Patients	27.15 (24.02)	77.13 (35.65)	38.17 (33.99)	<.01
	% with an MBBS Degree	0.43 (0.50)	1.00 (0.00)	55% (50%)	<.01
	Competence	–0.12 (1.12)	0.37 (0.95)	–0.01 (1.10)	<.01
Patient Characteristics	% Repeat Clients	37% (48%)	42% (49%)	39% (49%)	<.01
	% Not Young	45% (49%)	63% (48%)	53% (50%)	<.01
	% Male	52% (50%)	47% (50%)	50% (50%)	<.01
	Days patient has been sick (medium)	3.00	7.003		<.01
	Average Income of Patients who Visit	Rs. 8042 (60.26)	Rs. 5934 (2755)	Rs. 6979 (4796)	<.01
Outcome Variables	Average Effort Exerted	0.25 (0.93)	–0.34 (0.99)	0 (1)	<.01
	Poly-Pharmacy (Total number of medicines given)	2.84 (1.43)	2.36 (1.39)	2.63 (1.43)	<.01

Notes: The table shows characteristics of patients and providers as well as outcome variables separated across the public and private sector. Doctor characteristics are based on a census of providers carried out before the vignettes and direct clinical observation. Note, that "average patients" is the answer to a question in the census "On average how many patients do you see in a day in this location" and not the patients seen on the day of the observation (the census was always done in the same location as the observation). Age and tenure are both included since the doctor may have practiced in other locations before coming to the present clinic. Patient characteristics and outcome variables are interaction specific and based on the 4,108 observations of the clinical observation data. Care should be taken in interpreting the number of days question, since in 60% of cases, the doctor did not ask this question of the patient and the observation is missing. The "average income of patients who visit" is computed from the matched household-doctor data and represents the average per-capita annual consumption expenditure (using the abbreviated NSS schedule) of households who visit the specific doctor, weighted by the total number of visits over a 2 year period.

[a]NS: Difference not significant at 10% level. <.05: difference is significant at 5% and < .01 difference is significant at 1% levels of confidence.

Table 10.3: Practice, Competence

Panel A: Dependent Variable is Questions asked/examinations performed for diarrhea and cough in observation					
	(1)	*(2)*	*(3)*	*(4)*	*(5)*
Public doctor	–0.160 [0.014]a	–0.160 [0.014]a	–0.165 [0.015]a	–0.138 [0.023]a	–0.153 [0.023]a
General hospital	0.052 [0.015]a	0.042 [0.015]a	0.038 [0.015]b	0.027 [0.016]	0.066 [0.029]b
Vignettes performance		0.190 [0.025]a	0.188 [0.025]a	0.173 [0.026]a	0.159 [0.023]a
Constant	0.202 [0.010]a	0.153 [0.011]a	0.159 [0.018]a	0.204 [0.041]a	
Observations	4766	4766	4607	4394	4394
R-squared	0.04	0.06	0.06	0.06	

Panel B: Dependent Variable is Effort-in-Practice					
Public doctor	-0.809 [0.179]a	-0.845 [0.167]a	-0.757 [0.156]a	-0.759 [0.177]a	
General hospital	0.841 [0.189]a	0.708 [0.163]a	0.655 [0.155]a	0.661 [0.176]a	
Ability (MLE estimate)		0.210 [0.040]a	0.206 [0.037]a	0.210 [0.052]a	
Constant	0.379 [0.080]a	0.426 [0.077]a	0.212 [0.077]a	0.142 [0.228]	
Observations	3985	3985	3848	3778	
R-squared	0.20	0.24	0.35	0.35	

Panel C: Dependent Variable is Poly-Pharmacy					
Public doctor	–0.476 [0.211]b	–0.582 [0.209]a	–0.539 [0.205]a	–0.625 [0.220]a	
General hospital	0.344 [0.158]b	0.279 [0.156]	0.180 [0.147]	0.191 [0.169]	
Ability(MLE estimate)		–0.023 [0.072]	–0.020 [0.070]	–0.091 [0.072]	
Constant	2.386 [0.102]a	2.819 [0.104]a	2.210 [0.112]a	2.457 [0.385]a	
Observations	4307	4009	3860	3789	
R-squared	0.01	0.03	0.08	0.09	

Additional Patient Controls			X	X	X
Additional Practitioner Controls				X	X

Note: For Panel A, we use whether the provider performed each of 9 important tasks for patients presenting with diarrhea and cough without fever as the dependent variable (see text). Panel B uses Effort-in-Practice, constructed as the principal components score based on 6 variables C uses the total number of medicines given (either through direct dispensation or prescription) as the dependent variable. For Panel A, we use the predicted probability of asking each of these tasks in the vignettes as the measure of competence. The first 4 specifications are linear; the last is a random effects probit model. For Panels B and C, competence is the IRT score from the vignettes and all specifications are linear (Das and Hammer 2005). For all panels, patient characteristics include whether the patient is a repeat client and the age and gender of the patient. Provider characteristics include gender, age, qualifications and tenure in the current location. Finally, all specifications include a measure for the case-load, which is taken from the following question asked in a census of all providers completed previously, "On average, how many patients do you see at this location every day?" Regressions in Panel A are clustered at the provider-patient level and in Panels B and C at the provider level. Standard errors are in brackets. (b): Significant at 5%; (a): Significant at 1%.

Source: Money for Nothing—The Dire Straits of Medical Practice in Delhi, India; Jishnu Das and Jeffrey Hammer, The World Bank.

How far does the disparity arise between competence of doctors and their effort level for the patients in different income areas (poor, middle and rich)? Figure 10.4 is a decomposition of competence and overall effort by the average income of the neighborhoods that the provider practices in. Among doctors in the public sector, competence is close to, or higher than average. Providers in the private sector are less competent, especially in poor neighborhoods. Patterns of effort are the opposite–private sector practitioners exert effort that is close to or above the average; all public sector providers put in effort that is (far) below average. The reasons for poor delivered care are thus very different. The constraining factor on the quality of medical advice dispensed in low-income areas among private sector providers is low competence and among public sector providers, low effort. This difference underscores the importance of decomposing practice-quality variations into variations in competence and variations in effort.

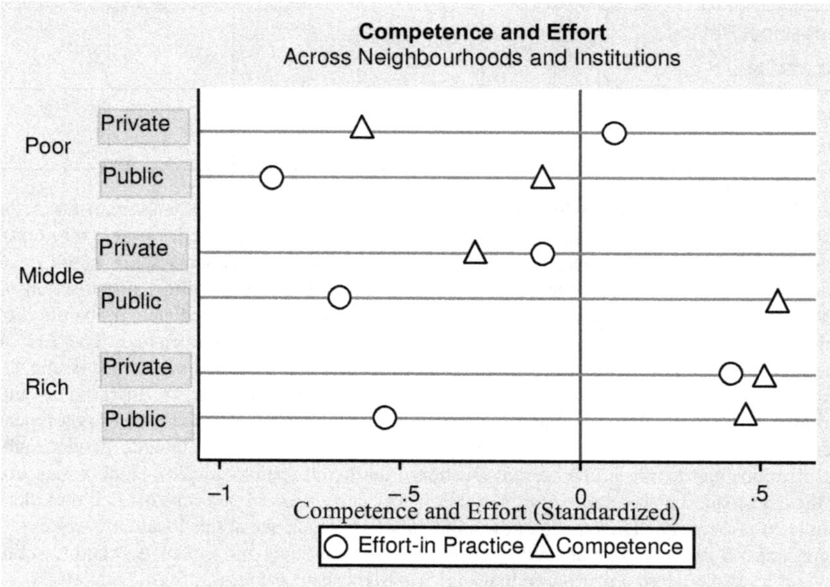

Fig. 10.4: Quality of Care by Neighborhood Income and Institutional Affiliation

Notes: The figure compares effort in practice to competence in the vignettes. The comparison is presented separately by the sector the doctor practices in and the average income of the neighborhood that she practices in. Both the competence and the effort index are standardized with mean 0 and variance 1, and therefore cannot be compared to each other. The figure shows that among the private sector, competence tends to be lower than average, but effort tends to be higher. In the public sector, competence is higher, but effort is (much) lower than average. The income measure is based on a consumption expenditure module administered to 40 randomly selected households in every neighborhood.

Source: Money for Nothing-The Dire Straits of Medical Practice in Delhi, India; Jishnu Das and Jeffrey Hammer, The World Bank.

Policy Model

The study however lends credence to the fact that that both non-MBBS and MBBS doctors exert much less effort in public medical services in relation to their private one to the patients in different income areas (poor, middle and rich). How is it possible to execute such a policy so that both non-MBBS and MBBS may not exert less effort in public medical services in relation to their private one to the patients in different income areas? It seems to be possible if government or institutions (principal) on behalf of the patients (beneficiaries), particularly patients having poor economic condition, insures the doctors (agent) against all risks. This seems to be desirable since agent is usually risk averse and principal is risk neutral. The neutrality of the principal may be judged by the fact that the principal might be indifferent to risk and there is no need to trade off incentives for risk sharing to help the patients receive full medical care from the providers' (doctors') end.

The model investigates the relationship between motivation, incentives and effort.

Why "principal-agent"?

- One party ("the principal": government) contracts with another party ("the agent": doctors) to perform some action or to take some decision in favor of patients (the beneficiaries).
- The agent has an information advantage – he knows something the principal does not know,
- The principal knows that the agent has this advantage (making it a potential handicap!).
- This effort is costly and the agent in question has to be motivated to put in effort.

By specifying different payments for different outcomes, the contract sets up incentives for the agent as he chooses an effort level. If under a given contract payments are larger for higher outcomes, and higher effort is more likely to produce higher outcomes (as is usually the case in these models), then the agent may be motivated to exert higher effort. If his expected utility from signing the contract and exerting some level of effort is larger than his reservation utility, he will sign the contract (this is the risk issue); if his expected utility from exerting high effort is higher than his expected utility from exerting any other level of effort then he will exert high effort (this is the incentive issue).

Let us illustrate the problem in analytical forms. Let us suppose that there are only a finite number of output levels (q_1, q_2, q_3, … q_n). Let v and r be two efforts that can be chosen by the agent out of some set of feasible efforts. These efforts influence the probability of occurrence of different output levels. Let us suppose that the probability that the output level q_i will occur if the agent chooses effort v(r) by π_{iv} (π_{ir}). Let $x_i = x(q_i)$ be the amount that the government pays if output level q_i is observed.

Then the expected profit of the principal (government), if agent (doctors) chooses action v, is

$$\sum_{i=1}^{n}(q_i - x_i)\pi_{iv} \qquad \ldots(1)$$

We know an optimal contracting arrangement can be defined as: a contract is optimal, if it maximizes the expected utility of the government for an expected utility of the agent subject to the condition that the agent finds it worthwhile to participate in the contract.

As cost of the agent for action v is c (v), then the agents expected utility less cost is expected utility less cost is

$$\left[\sum_{i=1}^{n}\{u(x_i)\pi_{iv}\}\right] - c(v) \qquad \ldots(2)$$

Here u: Von Neumann-Morgenstern utility function.

Two types of constraints are imposed in this self-enforcing contract (non-enforceability in the courts does not make contracts valueless. The contract acts in such a way that each party chooses to adhere to its term) – participation constraint and incentive comparability constraint.

Since the doctor is a utility maximiser, he/she will choose action u if

$$\left[\sum_{i=1}^{n}\{u(x_i)\pi_{iv}\}\right] - c(v) \geq \left[\sum_{i=1}^{n}\{u(x_i)\pi_{iv}\}\right] - c(r) \qquad \ldots(3)$$

and will choose effort r otherwise.

This constraint is referred to as the incentive compatibility constraint. The second type of constrain says that the agent may have other alternatives available that give him/her some utility $\bar{u}$. Then the participation constrain is

$$\left[\sum_{i=1}^{n}\{u(x_i)\pi_{iv}\}\right] - c(v) \geq \bar{u} \qquad \ldots(4)$$

The expected utility the agent gets from this job must be at least as great as the utility he/she could get elsewhere.

If the payment is based on effort rather than on output, then the principal is to determine the expected profit from each effort by the agent and then induce the effort that minimizes principal's expected profit. But as the efforts of the agent are hidden, payment to him/her cannot be a function of the unobservable effort (v, r). It can be made contingent on the observed output q_i. Attempt has been made to develop results along this line. Suppose that there is no incentive problem. However under the risk-neutrality assumption the principal is indifferent to risk and thus there is no need to trade off incentives for risk-sharing. In such a case the principal's (government's) optimization problem is

$$\sum_{i=1}^{n}(q_i - x_i)\pi_{iv}$$

subject to $$\left[\sum_{i=1}^{n}\{u(x_i)\pi_{iv}\}\right] - c(v) \geq \bar{u} \qquad \ldots (5)$$

where maximization is taken place over x_i.

In general, principal will want the agent to choose x_i to just satisfy the constraint so that

$$\left[\sum_{i=1}^{n}\{u(x_i)\pi_{iv}\}\right] - c(v) \geq \bar{u} \qquad \ldots (6)$$

The Lagrangian for this optimization problem is

$$L = \sum_{i=1}^{n}(q_i - x_i)\pi_{iv} - \lambda\left(\left[\sum_{i=1}^{n}\{u(x_i)\pi_{iv}\}\right] - c(v) - \bar{u}\right) \qquad \ldots (7)$$

where λ is the Lagrange multiplier.

Principal is risk-neutral because her expected profit is linear in x_i. Differentiating L partially with respect to x_i and λ, and setting the derivatives to zero, we have the first order conditions as

$$-\pi_{iv} - \lambda u'(x_i)\pi_{iv} = 0 \qquad \ldots (8)$$

$$\left[\sum_{i=1}^{n}\{u(x_i)\pi_{iv}\}\right] - c(v) - \bar{u} = 0 \qquad \ldots (9)$$

The first of the above conditions states

$$u'(x_i) = 1/\lambda \qquad \ldots (10)$$

a constant. i.e., x_i must be independent of i (x_i is a constant).

The contract fully insures the agent, who is risk averse, against all risks. The principal is risk neutral because his expected profit is linear in x_i implying that there is no need to trade off incentives for risk sharing. It seems to be an indication that the principal (government or institutions) has no need to trade off incentives for risk sharing to help the patients (beneficiaries—particularly patients having poor economic condition) receive full medical care from the agent (providers' or doctors') end. However, one of the significant limitations of this problem is that the principal knows the agent's utility function and incorporates this into the contract with agent. Despite limitations, the analytical theoretical works seem to suggest that in order to help the patients, particularly patients having poor economic condition, government may primarily provide the best incentive scheme to the doctors (equal for same categories of doctors) for their public medical services, but such an incentive scheme should not hardly differ from private medical services, if the latter desires to serve.

How is it possible to stimulate better performance in the public service? A systemic reality in many developing countries is that public service incentives are weak. There is the monetary side: Wages are too low and pay scales that at best are barely sufficient to live on, are not competitive with the private sector or do not compensate for postings to remote locations. Wages are too compressed, not reflecting the skills, training, and seniority of management positions as compared with low paid jobs. Further, non-monetary compensation and allowances play a major role in total compensation – benefits such as housing allowances, official cars, pensions, and other retirement benefits often form a large part of total compensation. These factors can contribute to a culture of absenteeism, alternative employment, rent-seeking and low productivity often compounded by a system of non-transparent benefits and allowances that discourage rather than encourage performance. Donor practices on salary supplements can further distort incentives, if not coordinated.

Conclusions

Incentive measures, such as salaries, secondary benefits, and intangible rewards, recognition or sanctions have traditionally been used to motivate employees to increase performance. A good incentive system will encourage employees to be productive and creative, fosters loyalty among those who are most productive, and stimulates innovation.

It is possible to execute such a policy in medical services so that both non-MBBS and MBBS doctors may not exert less effort in public medical services in relation to their effort in private medical services for their providing services for patients of different income groups in different areas. This study also suggests that the quality of health care received by patients varies due to two reasons: Difference in doctor's competence or differences in doctor's incentives. We find three patterns in the data. First, what doctors do is less than what they know; they should operate well inside their knowledge frontier. Second, competence and effort are complementary so that doctors who know more also do more. Third, the gap between what doctors do and what they know responds to incentives: Doctors in the fee-for-service in private sector are closer in practice to their knowledge frontier than those in the fixed-salary public sector. Under-qualified private sector doctors, even though they know less, provide better care on average than their better-qualified counterparts in the public sector. One hotly debated topic is the relative quality of providers in the private and the public sector. Some say that private providers are mostly "quacks" with little training and medical competence; others believe that the public sector is full of lazy doctors who do not work. As it turns out, each view has element of truth. These results indicate that to improve medical services, at least for poor people, there should be greater emphasis on changing the incentives of public providers rather than increasing provider competence through training. For the poor who visit low-quality public doctors and even somewhat lower-quality private practitioners, there are few easy solutions. Making public doctors in such areas more responsive to patient needs maybe possible through compensation schemes other than fixed salaries.

References

Besley, Timothy and Ghatak, Maitreesh [2003]: 'Incentives, Choice and Accountability in the Provision of Public Services', *The Institute of Fiscal Studies*, WP03/08, LSE.

Burgess, Simon, Propper, Carol, Ratto, Marisa and Tominey, Emma [2004]: *Incentives in the Public Sector: Evidence from a Government Agency*, University of Bristol.

Burgess, Simon and Ratto, Marisa [2003]: *The Role of Incentives in the Public Sector: Issues and Evidence*, Working Paper No. 03/071.

Davis, Jerome and Keiding, Hans [2008]: Incentive Contracts with Unobservable Competence Levels, *The Open Economics Journal*, 1, 47–54.

Delfgaauw, Josse and Dur, Robert [2006]: *Incentives and Workers' Motivation in the Public Sector*, Faculty of Economics, Erasmus Universiteit Rotterdam, and Tinbergen Institute.

Festré, Agnès and Garrouste, Pierre [2008]: Motivation, incentives and performance in the public sector.

Incentive Systems: [2006]: Incentives, Motivation and Development Performance: *A UNDP Capacity Development Resource,* Capacity Development Group, Bureau for Development Policy, United Nations Development Programme, November.

Miller, Nolan [2005]: Notes on the Principal-Agent Problem.

Rao, Ksujatha: Delivery of Health Services in the Public Sector, National Commission on Macroeconomics and Health, Government of India, New Delhi, web: http://whoindia.org/LinkFiles/Commission_on_Macroeconomic_and_Health_Delivery_of_health_services_in_the_Public_sector.pdf.

Institutional Issues in Economic Development: Rent Control and Argument for Institutional Change in the Third World Perspective

Pratanu Mitra

Introduction

The steady divergence in the growth rate of different economies has fuelled the development of a new school of development economics: the new growth theorists who contend that the existence of increasing returns to scale at the economy level makes capital investment more productive than in developing nations. This macroeconomic concept is rather counterintuitive to the conclusions of the neoclassical growth school. However, new growth theorists have sought to emphasize on the domination of coordination failure as a causal agent of chronic under-development. Distilling through the macro arguments, we eventually arrive at the failure of economic agents in their independent optimization behavior as the source of this coordination failure. This may be the failure of markets to function because of market imperfections, the absence of certain "prerequisites" which developed economies already possess and economic agents functioning in near perfect markets in such economies take for granted. These "prerequisites" may take any form-the legal structure, the bureaucratic environment, the corporate norms, the attitude of the people towards work, the informal constructs prevalent, or even the "way things are done" (for example, if you wish to start a business in Sicily, you need the blessings of the local *Mafioso*). Thus, a hazy picture seems to emerge from the above discussion—an underlying structure, or perhaps a fabric of an economy over which economic activities are carried out, namely the institutions or perhaps the nature of the institution prevalent in the economy. The author is concerned about the prevalent institution present in the owner occupied and rental housing market in Kolkata, a representative city of a developing economy, because the author has been in the city under discussion for a year and a half and has accumulated a wealth of experience regarding this particular market in a very short time. This paper tries to examine the impact of coordination failure due to existence of prevalent institutions in a developing owner occupied and rental housing market based on the empirics of a representative city in a developing economy.

Institutions: Definitions and Usage

Martin Weitzman, in a well-known article in 1994, distinguishes between transactions based on quantities and those based on prices. In quantity transactions, the prices of the exchanged goods and commodities remain wholly or partly indeterminate. Transactions may take on the character of quantity transactions in a modern economy when the uncertainty involving the costs and prices are high, magnified by asymmetries in information pertaining to the quality of the commodity or service being transacted. Institutions come into play as facilitators in quantity based exchanges. Institutions, Ashoka Mody (1993) remarks, are conduits for quantity-based transactions. Institutions thus defined emerge as rules, norms, and standards; organizations; and/or long-term relationships between economic agents that set into motion rules of exchange for a significant period in the future. Institutions inspire commitment in transacting parties, a commitment enforced by, and arising out of the expectation of continued interaction, doubly enforced by the fabric of informal contracts and constructs in place, which reduce deviations from established patterns of behavior in exchange. Institutions, therefore serve two fundamental roles, they alleviate severe asymmetries of information and uncertainty for the economic agent at the lower end of the information spectrum, agents who face severe income constraints, drastically reducing search and transaction costs. Institutions create binding commitments on the part of agents involved in exchange, and thus reduce chances of default in future. Institutions, in this context, are best considered mechanisms that allocate the scarce resources through "administrative" methods-preset norms of exchange that eliminate the need for the system of price signals. A point is to be made here regarding the functions of the state as institutions. State is a special, often powerful, and highly influential institutional form. However, if state as an endogenous institution enters the market, it may often end up being the sole power centre, thus concentrating the market, reducing allocative efficiency largely. It is useless to argue as to whether state action and performance in East Asian nation states can be replicated. Nevertheless, it is constructive to reflect upon the alternative forms of institutional arrangements which can perform the same allocation in ways to drastically cut down upon information imbalances, power imbalances, and in the process initiate institutional change—moving away from existing institutional structures which has resulted in the marginalization of the economically disadvantaged and merciless exploitation of the same.

The Problems: Its Elucidation and a Look into the Factors Promoting the Problems

A discussion of the problems in the owner occupied housing market will require a clarification of the nature of transactions that take place in this market, together with the influence of the favorable balance of relative power for the landlord on the same. It would be wrong and willful deception to say that prices and quantities were indeterminate. It is not so and a highly specialized and unique mechanism operates to fix price-output combinations. There is a process of search for rented accommodation on the part of the prospective tenant, a process aided by contacts, or peer help, and/or several newspaper advertisements. This brings the agents into contact and a transaction may or may not ensue. The determining factors are the location, the cost, and the facilities (e.g. located near a metro station, house cleaner services, laundry services, meal services-catering or nearby affordable restaurants, water availability, electricity). The householder will have every incentive to suppress information regarding defects and/or problems endogenous to the house and the tenant faces a problem of information asymmetry. He may feel an innate inability to proceed without greater information, but he is constrained heavily by time and a limited income. He cannot take recourse to ferreting out information from other tenants, if any, because they will have every incentive to be uncommunicative. An eviction is very costly for them in terms of transaction costs and the limited ability to adjust to a new psychosocial environment. These information problems can be analyzed in terms of the very famous *market for lemons model propounded* by Akerlof and a familiar reasoning brings us to the conclusion that the cream of the sellers exit the market. Depending on the fruitfulness of the process of search for the buyers and their alternatives the buyers will or will not complete the transaction. Note that sellers do not discriminate between buyers, they are confident in the belief that the excess demand in the market will throw up a large number of enquiries for their house and that it would not lie vacant. The point I wish to emphasize on here is: these transactions are mostly illegal; there are no formal records of the arrangement and the tenants are more often than not eligible for wrongful eviction. Over and above the householders' confidence that the perpetual pressure of the excess demand will throw up new and willing sacrificial goats, charge security deposits, thus covering their own losses in the event of the departure of the tenant without settlement of dues. However, the tenant is liable for eviction for a host of reasons, from not paying dues on time to the landlord's whim. The proxy black market fulfils a very essential resource allocation and the exploitation is a result of the market forces in this market. The market is imperfect because of relative asymmetries of information and imbalances of power owing to historical advantage. This paves the way for rent seeking behavior. Producers of this commodity find to their greater interest to coalesce to exploit these rent earning possibilities at the expense of the other interest group, the tenants, who have limited abilities to organize themselves because of conflict of interests and incentives. In short, their objectives are so constraint as to promote an undesirable outcome and constraints are so binding as to willfully accept this exploitation and move on. However, thresholds of human endurance may often be reached if the exploitation is too great and in that case, a unified tenant group will resort to the economics of the mob. To this end, the landlord finds his purpose served if he manages to prevent the unification of interests of the tenants—he has to resort to greater diversity in selecting tenants or he has to select tenants with greater constraints that would not permit such externalities. One could note in this regard the generation of restricted monopolies due to location. The suppliers are great in number but at given location the suppliers are limited and thus enjoy a greater degree of power. The quantity of housing supplied is thus a function of the location of the house. To this end, note the arbitrary and historical nature of the power generated from favorable location. The landlords have to pay out money to various local groups whose sole purpose of existence is protection. To this end this form of the market gives rise to corruption. Unabashed greed and avarice are spin-offs, as also are steadily deteriorating housing quality because of the perverse lack of incentives for the uncertain tenant to keep the room in good shape and the inability of the landlord to coordinate with the tenant. Thus, the outcome of a coordination failure is a long-term conversion of localities to slums. Lastly a system of third party transactions initiated by the landlord will often leave the tenants exploited on more than one front and looking for the person to blame.

The Structure of the Prevalent Institution

The institutional structure that resulted over the years after rent control legislation was passed is like a pyramid. The base may appear decentralized but it seldom is. The landlords have to pay for "protection" to the local leaders who in turn channel the money upwards. The links are more uncertain here. However, the landlords do not pay out of their pockets; they transfer this burden on their tenants who have no option but to pay if they are not to be evicted. They do not have much choice because of the uniformity of the choices facing them in the whole market. The irony is that the tenants are paying for the protection of the landlord's interests and the landlord is in turn mercilessly exploiting the tenants. This institution (sociologically devastating, marginalizing and economically disadvantaged agents) has evolved because the base has never stopped expanding. This has been the result of historic concentration of employment opportunities in the cities and urban gigantism and policies directed at exacerbating the same—unrestricted educational expansion and desperate attempts to expand the employment opportunities in the manufacturing and services sector in the cities. This has resulted in the transfer of advantage to landlords whose property is located (for historical reasons again) in regions where the tenants' employers have their productive units or students' have their educational institutions. An arbitrary distribution of income and wealth has taken place in favor of landlords and so according as they have been historically lucky. The theoretical explanation appears in the appendix.

Why is this Institution a Socially and Economically Undesirable One?

The institution has been systemically exploiting and sucking the lifeblood of those who can least afford it. These results in the removal from the market of the economically disadvantaged and their voices in the market are gradually becoming silent. This results in their demand requirements being phased out of the commodity market. Sociologically, this group of individuals has been systematically crushed and their accommodation problems have been reflected in their work effort. These people easily take to drink, drugs, and are slowly relegated to the dregs of society. The housing they inhabit slowly turn into slums because of the perverse incentive schemes which force the people as well as the proprietor to desist from improving their accommodation, in the face of uncertainty in their residence. The moral reasons are numerous; perhaps the greatest is their plight, which is coexisting with the affluent portions of the society as well as their increasingly affluent proprietors.

The Proposed Institutional Change and the Process for Achieving the Same

The proposed institutional change is very difficult to bring about because institutions have inertia. Since institutions are a result of information failures and uncertainty, they must be capable of evolving as circumstances and economic conditions change. The advocated change is in favor of decentralized institutional structures. Decentralization entails coordination and cooperative efficiency, but the costs of implementing decentralized institutions may be too large; so a case is created for government intervention, on which I am going to stress. Governments as institutions are often influential, but their involvements in the functioning of the market may raise unwarranted problems. Governments may act as to change the "fabric": the constraint structure or the rules of the game, so that new information and changing rules are absorbed quickly in the fabric of the economy, resulting in a flexible economy capable of processing and acting upon new information fast. The problem arises in the path of change, if individuals involved in governance are involved in various hierarchal characters of the institution. The exploitation of rent-seeking opportunities, and the coalescing of the interests of the group towards whom the balance of power is tilted, form institutions whose set-up costs are huge and which set in learning process that reinforces the existing institution. Behavioral pattern and patterns of coordination that thus emerge are based on rigidly set incentive structures, which are difficult to dislodge, again because of the tilt of power. Finally, the expectations are set up in such a way that reinforces the existing institutional framework. If this is the context in which I am asked to provide methods of institutional change, that change have to focus on breaking down the strongest elements of the existing institution, because the existing institution is socially inefficient, as has been discussed earlier, yet is persistent because of its self reinforcing tendencies and increasing returns to those in power. We need what is commonly referred to as political entrepreneurs, social preceptors, or change agents. I shall focus specifically on incremental change and the legal framework as the organization or institution that can upset the status quo. Their instructions carry the weight of law, which the ruling political party has to follow even if it goes against their interests. The ways in which this can be done are discussed next.

Creating Databases: Information dissemination and tackling information asymmetries is the first and foremost prerogative of any institution that comes into existence, because it is the existence of fragmented information pockets, which contribute to the augmentation of market power. The government in conjunction with a private entity or entities may go about compiling a database of rented accommodation vendors. However, this would require first that the agents providing housing on the black market gradually migrate to the legal market. However, this would be difficult because in the case of developing economies, it is often seen that agents with substantial market power act in conjunction with the state functionaries (bureaucrats) in creating an alternative institution, which sucks out the last drop of wealth from the economically disadvantaged. A set of incentives would be to focus on punitive action on the house owners who fail to join the database and on state functionaries who assist in evasion. However, this may prove counterproductive, in which the institution will have to focus on positive incentives, for example, tax exemptions on house repair, subsidies on the taxes already in effect and/or removal of whole sets of laws that make the houses already constructed illegal. Any of this would require overreaching powers and are controversial in that they leave room for further malfeasance. So the only approach left for the government to induce home-owners as well as not to depress investment in affordable realty would be to sanction the transactions, thus making them legal, but at the same time enabling some degree of protection for the tenants and removal of the uncertainty that is currently prevalent in their transactions. The creation of the database would require the institution to approach existing tenants for information and then incorporate this database making it available in the public domain and available to employers and educational institutions.

1. Rigid specification of the basic amenities should be provided to the tenants and regular regulation and supervision of the houses in the housing market by a team of investigators responsible directly to the committee in charge of the reforms in this institutional structure.

2. Creation of incentives need to be given for households already in the black market and for new households to enter into the legal market so that they may reduce tax liabilities and provide tax credit for renovation of housing.

3. There should be the abolition of the laws that exempt newly built houses from the purview of rent control and aggressively promoting investment in affordable housing.

4. Crackdown on offenders, seizures of property may be considered as a punitive action.

5. It needs to devise ways and means to reduce the huge excess demand that led to the systematic formation of the black market: passing a new piece of legislation making it mandatory for realty developers to construct affordable rented housing in accordance with the enormity of their existing contracts.

6. To educational institutions, it needs to abolish very high wage floors and stop indiscriminate issuance of licenses

Conclusion

Institutions set the rules and constraints, which facilitate the use of physical and human capital, to determine their productivity. They are a result of informational constraints, and human fallibility, so they must be able to change with the change in the broader fabric in which they are embedded. However, this change is very difficult to achieve because institutions have inertia, which are themselves a result of rigid incentive and hierarchical structures. Institutional change needs shocks to the status quo, something that political, social or change agents can provide. These are themselves institutions with competing incentive structures but have greater acceptances or credibility or power bases. Decentralized institutions are the result of very low inequalities in power and wealth distributions, and they provide the most efficient fabric over which market enabled transactions can take place. Optimal institutional structures are very difficult to realize in practice because of coordination and coexistence problems. Further research is indeed needed to provide an answer to the question: how have Western markets been able to extract part of the surplus that is generated due to inefficiencies and externalities and thus prevent the realization of rent seeking behavior to concentrate the market?

Appendix

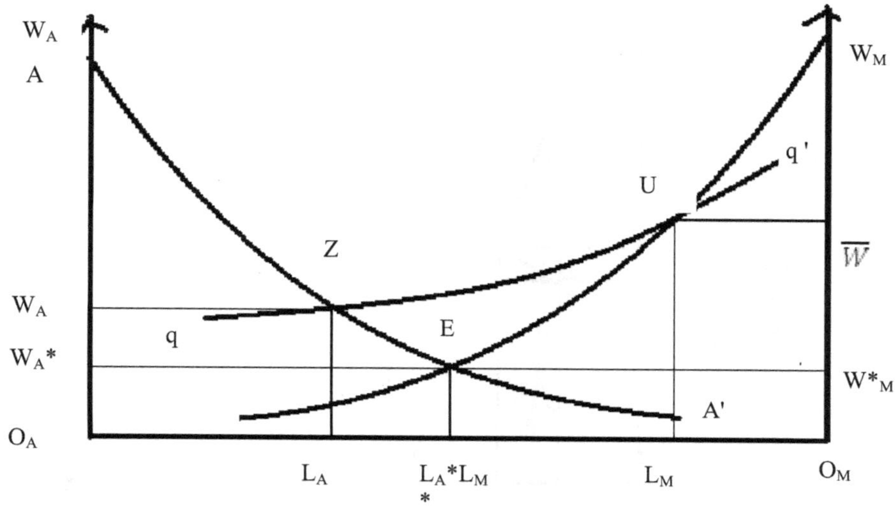

Fig. 1: The Harris Todaro Model of Rural Urban Migration

The Harris-Todaro model of rural urban migration explains the existence of underemployment equilibrium based on expected wage differentials. This model is central to the development of the pyramidal structure of an exploitative institution and the rigid incentive schemes and patterns of behavior as outlined in the paper. It explains how the indiscriminate educational expansion coupled together with the policies to increase employment rates and construction of new industries (resulting in urban concentration and gigantism) have led to the pyramid's base being ever expanding, forming a sustained source of excess demand. This excess demand and the historical nature of property distribution together contribute to the incentives to exploit the resulting institution. The rent control legislation has failed miserably because its Draconian provisions provide even more incentives towards the formation of an illegal market supported by entire corrupt bureaucratic and governance structures.

The formation of the black market: a comparative study of the mechanisms in the developing countries and those in the under-developed ones

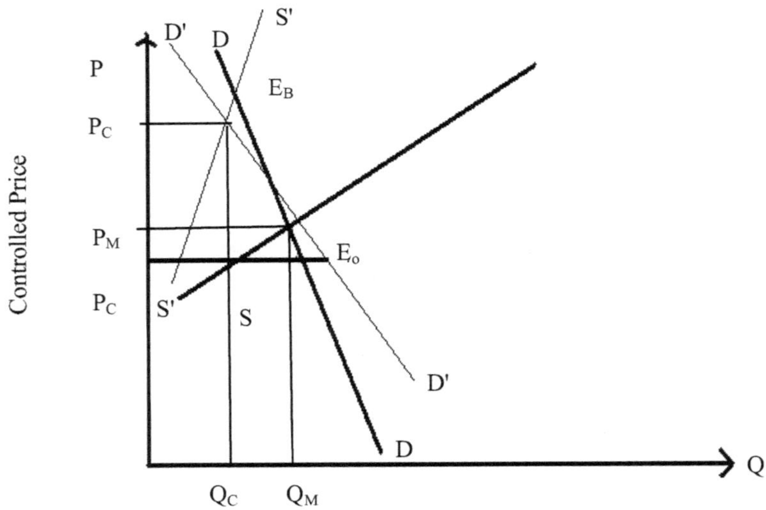

Fig. 2: Black Markets and their Formation because of Price Control

The development of the black-market and associated institutional, behavioral and coordination patterns as explained above is captured selectively in Fig. 2.

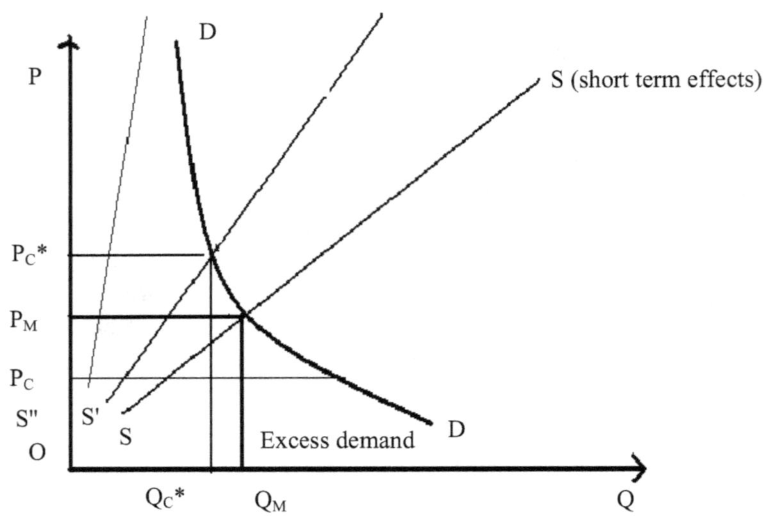

Fig. 3: Long and Short term Effects of Price Control in a Developed Economy

The effects of rent control in developed countries are less destructive in terms of the exploitation associated with it. Although key money, furniture provisions and voting for preferred candidates are often results of rent controls, but the presence of a well-developed legal structure and efficient policing and governance curtails direct exploitation. However, it may happen, as in Hong Kong, that misguided laws often lead to indiscriminate reconstruction of existing properties. On the other hand, the entire supply of rented apartments tending to zero, because of conversion of rented apartments to condominiums; and the removal of incentives to renovate existing structures because the profits accruing to property owners have been reduced greatly. Though the short-term aim of transfer of wealth to tenants from proprietors is achieved, in the end the effects are harmful even in developed economies. This goes on to show that misguided government policies often result in the origin of behavior patterns and institution development which lead to large imperfections in distribution of property and wealth and leads to huge social costs. The development of decentralized institutions, which facilitate transactions through the market system of price signals are often distorted and changed for the worse when policies aimed at curtailing market power in developed economies are brought about, because developed economies already have in place highly efficient structures—legal, bureaucratic or corporate which render markets efficient.

References

Akerlof, G. (1970): 'The Market for Lemons, Quality, Uncertainty and the Market Mechanism', *Quarterly Journal of Economics,* The MIT Press, 84(3), pp. 488-500.

Johson, D. (1951): 'Rent Control and Distribution of Income', *American Economic Review,* Papers and Proceedings, 41, May, pp. 571-582.

Lett, M. (1976): 'Rent Control, Concepts, Realities and Mechanism', *The Centre for Urban Policy Research,* New Jercy.

Marks, D. (1973): 'Public Choice and Rent Control', *Atlantic Economic Journal,* Vol. II, No. 3, pp. 63-69.

Mody, A. (1993): 'Making Institutional Choice' in P.K. Bardham, M. Chaudhuri and T.M. Krishnan (edited), *Development and Change: Essays in Honour of K.N. Rai,* Bombay, Oxford University Publication.

North, D. (1990): 'Institutions, Institutional Change and Economic Performance', *Cambridge University Press.*

Varian, H. (1994): 'A Solution to the Problem of Externalities when Agents are Well Informed', *American Economic Review,* 84, pp. 1278-1293.

Migration from Informal Urban to Rural Sector: An Approach to Developing Economy

Adway De, Puja Kankrania and Srijita Ghosh

Introduction

Since 2005, with the advent of new missions like Jawaharlal Nehru Urban Renewal Mission (JNURM) India moved in the path of 'urbanization' of her cities. The urbanization has been planned based on the philosophy of 'neoliberalism'. The concept of economic neoliberalism, based on the neoclassical theory of economics, refers to policies primarily focused on market activities. The concept of neoliberalism has now been applied to the planning of almost every country, especially in case of the Global south for rapid growth and 'urbanization' (The global south refers here mainly to the developing country of the world that has a mixed type of economy). The neoliberalising policy is characterized by universal back-tracking of the welfare state, dismantling of institutional constraints upon marketisation, increased commodification, shrinking of organized jobs and hyper exploitation of workers, downgrading of democratic rights earned through long-drawn struggles and a tremendous economic uncertainty. On the one hand it creates the 'utopia' of a free-market, liberated from all kinds of state interference to work most efficiently, but in practice it entails a coercive form of state intervention to facilitate market rule over a wider socio-spatial spectrum. It advocates from increasing constraints in planning and the political capacity of elected municipal government, deregulation and privatization of state-owned and state-provided services (mainly the basic services like housing, water, sanitation etc), withdrawal of state from urban development and making places for PPP projects specially in the infrastructure sector, expansion of space for elitist consumption and growing exposure to global competition. In one word it leads to a new form of governance that ostensibly suited a market-driven globalizing economy.[1] One of the main causes for adopting the neoliberalising policy by the developing nations is that the International Financial Institutions (IFIs) like IMF, WB, ADB—the main sponsors of the development projects—promote neoliberalism as a part of their ideological and functional sustenance. This intensifies unevenness in intra-urban and inter-urban development.

In a vision of making 'world class cities' sufficiently investment-friendly, acceptable to credit rating agencies and help them emerge as geostrategic points to further neoliberalism, the Indian Central Government in December, 2005 launched its largest post-independence urban planning initiative. With the advent of this project all the previously existing urban projects like National Slum Development Programme, *Swarna Jayanti Sahakari Rozgar Yojana*, *Valmiki-Ambedkar Aawaas Yojana* (for housing the socially marginalized urban poor), and the National Transport Policy were clubbed with the JNURM project. The mission identified the gap between disproportionately fast pace of urban growth and urban infra-structural development as the primary evil to the development process. So, the mission mainly focused on the infrastructural development of Indian cities. Under the mission, 63 Indian cities, 7 category A or mega cities, 28 category B or metro cities and 25 category C or urban agglomeration, would be 'urbanized'. The mission is classified into two sub-missions. Sub-mission A is entitled for Urban Infrastructure and Governance (UIG) accounts for 65% of the total fund. Under the Ministry of Urban development this sub-mission would deal with roads, transport, associated infrastructure, water supply, sanitation and beautification. Sub-mission B accounting 35% of the total fund would provide Basic Services to the Urban Poor (BSUP), under Ministry of Urban Employment and Poverty Alleviation (MUEPA). Slum improvement, rehabilitation of the displaced, access to basic services and housing projects for the urban poor come under this head.

Some basic features of the mission are the following:

- Privatization and commercialization of basic services through public-private partnership model and this may lead to user fees for these basic services.
- Liberalization of land and real estate market. The mission almost made it 'mandatory' for the states to repeal the Urban Land (Ceiling and Regulation) Act, 1976 (ULCA) that led to release of huge quantity of land in the urban market.
- Development of mortgage market and provision of 100% FDI in the housing and real estate.
- Bringing the urban poor in the orbit of pay-&-use framework.

Given this policy of 'urbanization we want to examine the effect of this structural change on the urban poor, especially those living in the slum areas.[2] According to 2001, census 24.13% of total population lives in slums in the major cities of India, the slum-to-total population in three major cities are 54.06 (Mumbai), 18.74 (Delhi) and 32.48 (Kolkata). So, the slum population being a major part of each of the cities we should examine the effects of new policies on them. Our main objective is to study whether the mission would improve their standard of living and hence lead to the development of this section reducing the intra-urban inequality or this would lead to further reduction in their standard of living. In most of the cities the urban local bodies are taking initiatives to provide better services to the slum dwellers but what is the actual developmental impact on them needs to be studied.

One point needs to be mentioned here is that with the abolishment of ULCA and the increasing process of urbanization, the slums, occupying considerable areas at the heart of the cities, have become vulnerable. In many cases the slums are being demolished and the people are provided with better housing opportunities majorly in the outskirts, but there still remains large number of slums in every city. So, the slums in every cities is, no doubt, a acute problem in the rapid process of urbanization .This paper is an attempt to examine the benefit of migration from urban to rural sector for the large number of poor people living in slums in every city. We first try to examine the theoretical underpinnings in analytical forms and then try to justify the same by empirical facts particularly in Indian perspective.

The Theoretical Underpinnings

Let us consider a two-sector model, namely urban and rural sector.[3] We did not take formal urban sector into account in this framework. The real wage and standard of living for single individual in the formal urban sector are always higher than that of urban informal sector or rural sector. Our analysis is confined into urban informal sector and rural sector based on the consideration of neoclassical market model where individuals are optimizers and take decisions based on relative benefit and cost analysis. So, economic activities like migration will be based on its cost-benefit judgment by the single individual. As we are more concerned about the urban poor, our analysis will be entirely based on the economic decision of this section of people.

In executing the theoretical underpinnings we assume the following:

1. The urban money wage of (W_U) of an individual in the informal sector is much higher than rural money wage wage (W_R), i.e., $W_U > W_R$.
2. Average price level in the rural sector is lower than urban sector ($P_R < P_{UI}$).
3. We assume that despite the fact that there has been a significant decrease of real wage of an individual in the informal urban sector, the real wage of urban individual in the informal sector is still higher than that of rural one. Mathematically, W_U/P_{UI} would be higher than W_R/P_R, where P refers to the average price level.
4. The cost of living for an individual in informal urban sector is higher than that of rural sector.
5. The standard of living of an individual in the rural sector is much higher compared with informal urban sector (real wage is not the only ingredient of standard of living).
6. We assume that there exists large amount of disguised unemployment in both informal urban sector and rural sector.
7. The cost of migration of an individual from urban (rural) to rural (urban) sector is c.

Now, based on the model if we analyze the present situation of Indian cities it seems to appear that with the advent of new policies households, irrespective of whether or not provided housing accommodation, would need to pay higher than they used to pay at past for the basic services like water, sanitation etc., even the houses are not provided free of cost for the rehabilitants. Individuals in most cases have to make a lump sum down payment even before entering into the new house. The end result is that the cost of living of an individual in the informal urban sector would usually increase, and the standard of living would decrease.

One of the possible solutions might be in the following lines: if housing accommodation of an urban individual working in the urban informal sector is established in the rural areas along with better transport structure so that he may be employed in the urban areas but lives in rural areas, it may not decrease the standard of living of the urban individual working in the urban informal sector. In such a case the c must be kept as low as possible. Such a migration for an urban individual working in the informal sector is possible so long as the standard of living of an urban individual working in the urban informal sector having housing accommodation in the rural areas will be equal to the standard of living of a rural individual working in rural sector having housing accommodation within rural sector.

Now most of the people who live in the slums of the city are engaged in the unorganized labor sector. The unorganized labour sector is characterized by excess supply of labour. So, migration of these laborers won't much affect the employment scenario of the cities. Besides, many employment opportunities of these people, at present, have come to an end with the closure of small scale manufacturing and retail units, regulations against informal workers, hawkers, waste pickers etc. In the case of shrinking of employment opportunities, the urban wage (W_U) may also reduce considerably. Then the migrated poor would possibly try to engage in the rural sector leading to even worse situation in the already exploding rural labor market.

In this context we would analyze the development issues also. If after the migration the real wage (real wage minus cost of migration) is less than the urban real wage before migration then the standard of living of the concerned group will fall. This is a loss to the development impact as a whole. Another point is that the freedom of choice of where to live is a fundamental right to every individual.[4] If the policy influences the preference pattern and 'compels' the individual to migrate, then it would create a distortion in the economy as well as violation of fundamental right.

Empirics

Now, using some empirical facts we would try to justify our theoretical argument. For that we would first take the case of Nonadanga. Then we would examine some data on slums in Delhi. Data in support of our claims regarding the abolition of land ceiling act and marginalization of poor by contracting their employment opportunities would also be presented.

Nonadanga

On both sides of the railway tracks from Ballygunge (South Kolkata) to Budge Budge (suburb of Kolkata) there were several thousand families—the residents of Gobindapur Rail Colony—who were living there for generations. When the railways decided to evict them, about 1700 of these families were ceremoniously rehabilitated in Nonadanga beside the EM Bypass Road.[5] With a vision of improving the urban environment in outer areas of Kolkata, protecting environment from adverse developmental impact and other developments the Kolkata Environmental Improvement Project (KEIP) and KMDA took a rehabilitation projects for people living in the slums situated by the East Canal in 2006 financed by the Asian Development Bank. Nonadanga was one of the moujas under the project. According to KMDA report around 14,240 slum populations were involuntarily brought under this project. But the primary survey of Nonadanga Bandhab Samiti reports reveal that almost 50 families were not rehabilitated until September, 2009. We can't trace these families in the official documents; probably they have shifted (or migrated?) to some other places.

In the rehabilitation project total households have had to incur 20% of the total cost of the project. This means each family had to give Rs. 24,000.[6] Initially each family had to give Rs. 5,000 for the new housing. The basic infrastructure was miserable there- they had to live there without proper drinking water, sanitation or health and education services till 2009. Municipality promised to arrange basic amenities for the residents over there, but after the completion of the project the residents co-operative would have to take the responsibility of these services. This leads to increase in the cost of living and a subsequent fall in the standard of living of the residents.

It is not clear from the primary data whether all the families are actually rehabilitated in the new housing and we can't trace where almost 50 families were shifted who were living in temporary houses beside the canal. Though it is not clear whether people have migrated from the place, one thing can be said that in near future families may migrate from these new housing complexes to elsewhere. Basically KMDA is willing to make a developed 10 acre land available for IT/ITES industries. The place is strategically located within the city, on EM Bypass, with all requisite infrastructures. HSBC Data Processing Centre, Rolta and HCL Infosystems Pvt. Ltd. are companies willing to set up their centers in this site. May be that is the reason why the slum dwellers were relocated from their original position.

Delhi

Among the other cities of India, Delhi experienced both direct slum demolition and costlier basic amenities. Between 1975 and 1977, seven lakh people were evicted to the fringes of Delhi under the order of DDA. In 2000, fifteen thousand *jhuggis* (slums are commonly known as *jhuggis* in Delhi) were demolished and seventy five thousand people were displaced, most of whom were not replaced. In 2004, Yamuna Pushta—

the biggest slum cluster of Delhi—was demolished, uprooting over 30,000 families. Only a quarter of the evicted got alternative plot in the resettlement colonies on the outskirts of the city. On 29 March, 2006 one thousand two hundred *jhuggis* were demolished at Nangla Machi, Delhi and so on.

The alternative sites provided to the displaced are not 'free of cost'. The Draft Annual Plan 2000-01 of urban department of the Government of National Capital Territory of Delhi mentioned that in case of relocation the relocated 'licensee' would pay an interest free cash security of Rs. 5,000, a license fee of Rs. 200 per year to be charged for 10 years in the first instance, and Rs. 1,000 as relocation charges to the concerned department before taking possession. So, a slum dweller would have to pay a total of Rs. 8,000 even before moving to the relocation site. Needless to say, if a family is unable to pay this amount before rehabilitation they would be forced to migrate.

The basic amenities are charged in the relocated sites. In Bawana they charge for using the public toilet—Rs. 1 to use the toilet, Rs. 2 to bathe, and Rs. 5 to wash clothes. An impoverished family of five would thus be expected to pay Rs. 20 per day for essential. This clearly increases the cost of living of the poor families. It wouldn't possibly be irrelevant to mention here that the famous Arjun Sengupta committee report remarked that almost 70% of the total population in India is able to make expenditure less than Rs. 20 per day.[7]

The Olga Tellis Case

The Olga Tellis was an example of how the employment opportunities were destroyed by the urbanization policy. In 1981 the chief minister of Maharashtra announced that all pavement dwellers in the city of then Bombay were to be evicted forcibly and deported to their respective places or origin or removed to sites outside the city. The case was brought in front of the court as a PIL in response to the announcement. The demolitions were stayed by an order of the Bombay High Court. It was contended that pavement and slum dwellers resided near their places of work. Evicting them would also mean taking away their livelihood, and consequently their right to work and right to life (conferred by Article 21).[8]

Case Studies Related to Abolition of ULCRA

As mentioned earlier, one of the major causes of slum displacement as a part of the urbanization process is to make more lands available in the urban land market that would be used to build real estate or consumption centers, like shopping mall, multiplexes etc. for the urban rich as slums are possible source of land in the urban market. The data collected from and around Kolkata supports this view. Calcutta riverside project is coming up on 262 acres of land that aims at housing a nine-hole golf course, high end villas (flats cost around Rs. 1.11 crore!), Condominium hotels, IT parks etc. Similarly 400 acres of land formerly belonging to the Hindustan Motor Limited in Uttarpara is going to house another large residential project. The Joy Engineering works near Jadavpur is replaced by a 35-storey residential tower and a 10,00,000 square feet mall.[9] Within two years (as for 2009) 12 more multiplexes is going to build in Kolkata and Howrah and this will lead to further marginalization of urban poor through both displacements and shrinking of job opportunities.

Conclusions

From the theory and empirics used here we can conclude that there would possibly an urgent need of an urban-rural migration in India as we have been increasing the process of urbanizing. Having studied the benefit of migration from urban to rural sector for the large number of poor people living in slums in every city in a developing economy, this study suggests that migration for an urban individual working in the informal sector is possible so long as the standard of living of an urban individual working in the urban informal sector having housing accommodation in the rural areas will be equal to the standard of living of a rural individual working in rural sector having housing accommodation within rural sector. To make this programme more effective, better structure of communication with least cost needs to be affordable to the migrants. Added to it, infrastructure regarding housing accommodation, sanitation and other related facilitates should be provided to the migrants with least cost. Moreover, rural employment opportunities should be generated based on the local resources. This can be done by investing in proper infrastructural projects in the rural sector that would mostly involve the local residents. In that case demand for labour in the rural sector increases, hence the rural wage. Now if the development in the rural sector is made in such a manner as it should not affect the standard of living of the migrants, who are now a part of the rural population, then the gap of the standard of living between these two groups vanishes. In this case again the individuals become indifferent between commuting to urban sector for work and working in the rural sector.

As the rural sector in India is characterized by excess supply of labor, mostly unskilled, so labor-intensive industries would be more suitable for the rural sector. There exists a huge infrastructural difference between rural and urban sector; so infrastructural projects will simultaneously improve the labor demand and decrease the urban-rural inequality to some extent. One of the major causes of rural underdevelopment is that goods that are produced in the rural sector, mostly agricultural goods, are generally low-priced; so industries that use such agro-based products and increase the value of agricultural products are more suitable for the rural sector. It is worthwhile that highly capital-intensive technology-based industries, which involve majority of skilled workers, are not suitable for the rural sector. This would neither increase the wage for the rural people nor would increase their standard of living. In this context we can consider the case of Singur, where the automobile and its ancillary all industries were mostly capital-intensive: hence this won't be able to change the rural employment position.

Notes

1. Swapna Banerjee-Guha, Neoliberalising the Urban, *Economic and Political Weekly*, June 5, 2009.
2. According to The Slum Areas (Improvement and Clearance) Act of 1956 an area is declared as slum area if the buildings in that area in any respect unfit for human habitation or if they are detrimental to safety, health and morals.
3. Here we define urban area as the cities where the urbanization projects are undertaken and rural area consists of both the agrarian economy and the suburbs, which is excluded from these policies.
4. Human Development Report (2009): Overcoming Barrier: Human Mobility and Development, *UNDP*.
5. Sanhati.com
6. Kolkata Environment Improvement Project, Project Number: 29466, September 2009, www.keip.in.
7. Abandon (2008): *Displacement and Development*, Perspectives, Chapter VI, Urban Displacement.
8. *Ibid*.
9. Swapna Banerjee-Guha, Neoliberalising the Urban, *Economic and Political Weekly*, June 5, 2009.

Empirics of Development Status in West Bengal: An Inter-District Study during 1980–2000

Aparajita Dasgupta, Indrani Basu and Debnarayan Sarker

The objective of this paper is to make an assessment of the overall status of development in the state of West Bengal with a special stress on the inter-district disparities. Though it is difficult to capture the different variants of development in a single framework, this study attempts to provide an overall view of the level of development of the 19 districts through an aggregate score and thereby ascertain the relative position of the districts in the development panorama. This assessment will help us in deciding inter-sectoral as well as inter-regional financial allocations within the state, and enable to identify areas that require particular policy attention. The performance of the districts in terms of alternative criteria of development is therefore essential in judging the efficacy of development administration in the state and in identifying the districts by criteria, which still require special attention from the state government. More disaggregated district level analysis would surely help us identify the gaps that still exist in our development efforts. The use of alternative criteria helps us in identifying the extent of deprivation or otherwise by these criteria in different districts, such that the scope for further public action in such areas or activities can be identified. For example, a district may be fairly advanced compared with others in terms of agricultural productivity but not in terms of access to sanitation, health care or educational facilities and therefore ranking score by alternative criteria of development would indicate the need for special emphasis in certain well specified direction.

The present study has been undertaken with the following specific objectives:

- To assess the overall status of development in the state of West Bengal between 1980-81 and 2000-01 on the basis of certain selected indicators.

- To locate the relative position of the different districts with reference to specific area of development, for example, social development, health and education.
- To develop a composite district development index and obtain a comprehensive development ranking of the districts taking into consideration both economic and social dimensions.

The present study is divided into five sections. Section 1 presents the data source. The methodology of the empirical analysis related to compound growth rate, composite index and principal component analysis appears in the appendix. The regression results are contained in the endnotes. Section 2 assesses the position of West Bengal in the national context. The socio-economic aspects of development are highlighted here. We also study the time trend and growth rate based on PCI (Per Capita Income) and SDP (State Domestic Product). In section 3, we analyze the inter-district comparison of development on various socio-economic issues. This section also deals with the overall ranking of the districts based on the composite indices. Concluding observations are portrayed in the last section.

1. Data Sources

As there exists dearth of authenticated published data for the districts, they had to be culled out from diverse sources. The data used in this study have been drawn from various issues of Statistical Abstract and Economic Review published by the government of West Bengal. District Statistical Handbook (DSH), Government of West Bengal, contains useful information. These publications provide block-disaggregated data apart from district level data. DSH contains information on different matters relevant to development of a district –for example, roads maintained by PWD and local bodies, small industries, villages electrified etc. Census Reports on various issues provide important data. The information on literacy rate, sanitation coverage, pacca road connectivity, rural water supply coverage of villages are taken from these reports. WBHDR 2004 (West Bengal Human Development Report) is of great use for the present study.

2. West Bengal in the National Context

Comparisons in terms of economic growth and human development between West Bengal and other states of India shows that West Bengal is somewhere in the middle of all Indian states. The West Bengal Human Development Report (HDR) brings out a mixed picture of the current state of human development in West Bengal with some important successes and also some areas of inadequate achievement as well as certain emerging problems.

Per capita State Domestic Product (SDP) in West Bengal in the late 1990's was just above the national average. The World Bank, in its report published in February 2002, adjudged West Bengal as one of the two States in India with the strongest focus on growth. The State's performance has been impressive in recent years. Industrial production has grown at an annual rate of 4.6 per cent. The average annual growth of State domestic product (SDP) during the Ninth Plan stands at 7.2 per cent as against 5.4 per cent in the case of the gross domestic product (GDP) of the country during the same period. Fig. 13.1 compares the SDPs of the year 1997-98 between the states in India.

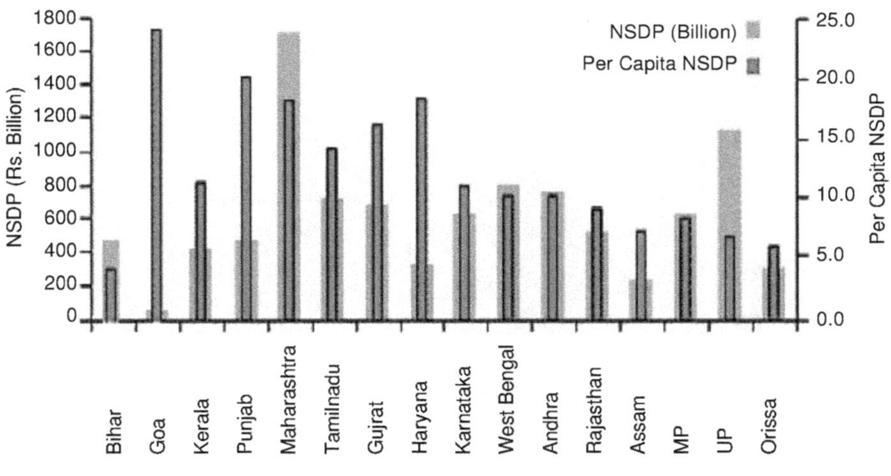

Fig. 13.1: Comparison of State Domestic Product 1997–98

Fig. 13.2 shows per capita SDP in 1990-91. From the above figure it is evident that West Bengal holds a moderate position in terms of per capita SDP, with a rank of about 6 among the 15 important states. According to the planning commission, the incidence of poverty in West Bengal in 1999-2000, at 27% of the population below the poverty line, was only marginally higher than the national average of 26%. In terms of basic household amenities, West Bengal's performance tends to be lower than the national average. Electrification has proceeded more slowly (33% coverage in 1991) than in the rest of India (42%). Literacy and education indicators in West Bengal are well below than expected values. Aggregate literacy rate at 69% in 2001 was marginally above the national average of 65%. Health indicators suggest a very mixed performance – infant mortality rates are among the lowest in India, child mortality rates are also relatively low, and life expectancy is higher than the national average. Nutrition indicators are rather poor with higher incidence of anemia among young children than for India as a whole.

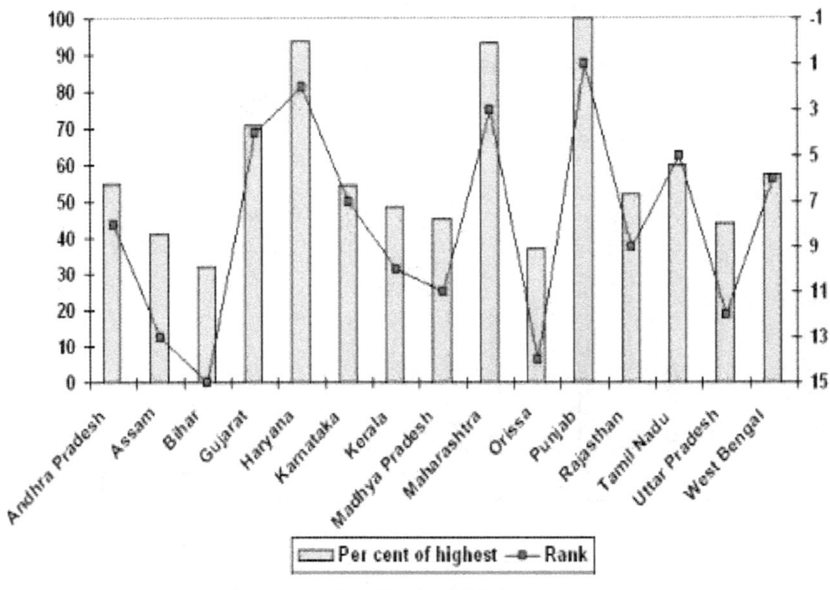

Fig. 13.2: Per Capita SDP in 1990–91

3. Socio-Economic Aspect of Development in West Bengal

The WBHDR analyses two major public initiatives, which have characterised the State for the last 26 years, i.e. land reforms and decentralisation and has examined their effects on human development. Further, it attempts to understand the reasons as to why the positive effects of these initiatives have not been more pronounced on human development attainments.

Not only does West Bengal dominate India in land distribution but there is greater protection afforded to cultivating tenants than anywhere else in India. It is the only State to have held regular elections to the panchayats every five years, and these panchayats have been given greater administrative responsibilities and become important instruments of social mobilisation. The panchayats played an important role in implementing and monitoring the land reforms, and these land reforms created a social dynamic which ensured that the panchayats have been more democratic and socially representative than in most other States. Both of these processes then contributed to the increase, first of all, in agricultural production, and then in other small-scale production.

The West Bengal Human Development Report 2004 explores the implications of this strategy for economic growth, human development and the overall conditions of life of the people, asks why the positive effects have not been more pronounced, and considers the factors constraining human development in the State at present.

The report present a mixed picture of the current state of human development in West Bengal. On the positive side, there are definite and important achievements which are possibly unmatched in any other State of India. The substantial progress in land reforms as well as the early and sustained efforts at increasing people's participation in government through panchayats provided important forces making for increased productive capabilities in agriculture and small-scale production, greater empowerment of the poor, more equity in basic consumption patterns and greater voice for ordinary people, including workers in urban and rural areas, women and Scheduled Caste/Scheduled Tribe groups. These initiatives and the social forces they generated also provided much greater human security, helped the people of the State to avoid the spread of communal and caste-based disharmony that were part of its history and recently became more prevalent in other parts of India.

In the last two decades, the State has experienced relatively rapid economic growth, compared with the rest of the country, and more importantly, unlike most of the rest of the country, this growth has been small producer-led in all the major sectors. The most remarkable acceleration of growth occurred in agriculture, as the State that was described as being in an "agrarian impasse" in the early 1980s, experienced the highest rates of crop output growth in the country. In the last two decades, the annual rate of growth in food-grain production in West Bengal was 4.1 per cent as against an average of 2.5 per cent for all major States. This was led by small peasants as land reforms reduced several institutional fetters to growth, making for more efficient use of land as well as greater utilisation of groundwater resources.

Industrial growth, which accelerated from the mid-1990s, was dominated by small-scale unregistered manufacturing units in rural areas, which was more than doubled in number and employment though the formal manufacturing sector stagnated. As in the rest of India, the services sector grew at the fastest rate, reflecting a combination of positive dynamism and with high productivity. Figure 13.3 shows the trend of rising investment in West Bengal for the time period 1961-2000.

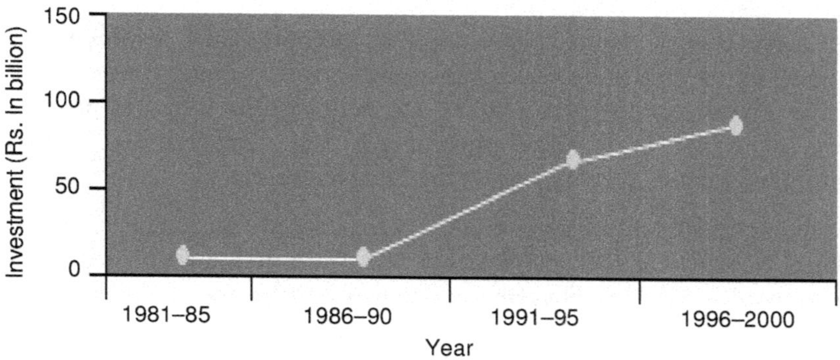

Fig. 13.3: Investment in West Bengal

The puzzle is that such small producer-led growth nevertheless failed to generate adequate productive employment to meet the requirements of the growing labour force. This may be why progress in terms of some important human development indicators has been less than could be expected given these other achievements. The lack of adequate productive employment opportunities is probably the most pressing socio-economic problem in the State. The paid employment of women, which was already low by national standards, has diminished further in relative terms in the recent past. The spread of literacy and education has been slow, and the failure to achieve universal primary education is a major disappointment. Inequalities of access to education according to gender and social category, and by region, are still considerable, despite recent attempts to reduce these imbalances.

Similarly, while health and nutrition outcome indicators indicate a greater degree of equity across income groups than other States, gender differences remain important and there are lacunae and inadequacies in public delivery systems for both preventive and curative health. In both education and health, the quality of public service delivery remains a serious concern. Environmental conditions, especially water and air pollution and land degradation, are of growing concern. Regional imbalances within the State continue to be significant.

Macroeconomic processes such as the stagnation of employment opportunities, the adverse effects of trade liberalisation on small producers, the collapse of rural institutional credit and the effective disintegration of the Public Distribution System, had direct and indirect effects upon the conditions of life and human development in the State.

Efforts have been made in both health and education, through, for example, the alternative schooling created by the Shishu Shiksha Kendras as well as the proposed schemes for panchayat-controlled health units rather than department-controlled primary health centres. These schemes typically involve much lower remuneration and non-permanent contracts to service deliverers such as teachers and health workers, which is why they can be undertaken at much lower cost. While they may be necessary transitional measures, they are far from the ideal solution, which would involve more resources being made available to locally accountable public service delivery systems.

Overall Ranking of the Districts

The present study seeks to examine inter-district disparities in the field of agriculture, infrastructure, education, social development in West Bengal. Composite indices have been prepared for the districts in these fields and ranked accordingly. Kolkata is deliberately omitted from the analysis because of excessive Kolkata-centricity of all our development projects; it is truly an outlier. Inclusion of kolkata artificially suppresses inter-district variations. Analysis has not been possible taking all 19 districts into account, because of unavailability of relevant disaggregated data for this study.

In order to construct the Agricultural Composite Index (ACI) we consider the following variables:

CI : Crop intensity (1999)

I : Percentage of Irrigation coverage (1999)

FC : Fertiliser Consumption (1999)

CB : Commercial bank branches (2000-01)

PAC : Per hectre availability of Agricultural Credit (in ₹)

RC : Pacca road connectivity in villages (1991 census)

VE : Villages Electrified (1999)

LR : Literacy Rate (1999)

L : Livestock (1999)

AT : Agricultural Tractor (1999)

SMY : Sub-Market Yard (1999)

Y : Food grains productivity (kg/hectare) (2000-01).

Various studies have emphasized the role of infrastructure development for promoting economic growth, mainly in the context of the development of the industrial sector. In one of the early studies in this area covers period 1960-1986. Barnes and Binswanger examine the impact of rural electrification through private investment in electric pumps on agricultural productivity. According to them, investment in electric pumps led to expansion of land under cultivation and allowed double and multiple cropping and increased profitability of use of high yield variety of seeds and other purchased inputs. Impact of rural infrastructure is conceived as a two-stage process. First, access to infrastructure has an impact on farming practices. Second, adoption of new farming practices including hybrid seeds and fertilizers in turn have an impact on agricultural yields. Using the methodology of II (Appendix) we get the following ranking of the districts according to the calculated agricultural composite index.

Table 13.1: Rank of the Districts According to Agricultural Composite Index

District	*Composite Index*
Midnapur	1.834510586
Burdwan	1.37172273
Hoogly	1.052530014
Bankura	0.482715456
24 pgs (n)	0.295494888
Nadia	0.164321804
Birbhum	0.12174121
Murshidabad	–0.081100315
Malda	–0.388672891
24 pgs (s)	–0.444616946
Howrah	–0.463995784
Dinajpur (n & s)	–0.480690011
Cooch Behar	–0.740355519
Jalpaiguri	–0.750811441
Purulia	–0.752966633
Darjiling	–1.219077979

As may be seen from table 13.1, that Midnapur, Burdwan, Hoogly are high rank holders while Darjeeling, Purulia and Jalpaiguri are lagging behind. To identify the major factors influencing agricultural productivity, productivity of food grains (PTY) is regressed on cropping intensity (CI), percentage of irrigation coverage (IRG) and fertilizer consumption (FC) separately for the year 1995-96 and 2000-01. Under the food grains, paddy, wheat, vegetables, cereals and pulses are included. The estimated regression equation appears in the endnotes (i).

From the estimated regression equations it is observed that irrigation (IRG) is the single most important factor in explaining agricultural (food-grain) productivity. Though contrary to our expectation cropping intensity has a negative sign; here the t-value is very insignificant indicating the acceptance of the null hypothesis of absence of relationship. The F value of the overall regression is significant at 5% level. We observe that in 2000-01 the picture improved marginally. The coefficient of fertilizer consumption (FC) gained in statistical significance, though IRG still remains to be the largest influence. The R^2 value has also increased from 56% to 75% and the F-value for the regression equation becomes significant at less than 1% level.

To carry out a stability test of the regression parameters across the two time points, a chow test (#1) is attempted with a pooled regression along with the previous ones. The pooled regression results also appears in the endnotes(ii). It is found from the pooled regression results that the observed value is less than the critical value which signifies the absence of any structural break in the agricultural front.

To determine the composite index of the districts in the infrastructural front, we use the same methodology which appears in the appendix. Here the dependent variable is Per Capita Income (PCY) and the independent variables are indicators of infrastructure development. Infrastructure facilities are in the nature of intermediate inputs that increase efficiency of other inputs. Their availability in adequate quantity and quality reduces input costs and raises profitability, thus, permitting higher level of output, income and employment.

Indicators of infrastructure development across districts are considered as follows:

x_1 : Length of surfaced roads maintained by PWD and ZP in km (1998)

x_2 : Pacca road connectivity in villages (1991 census)

x_3 : Length of unsurfaced roads maintained by PWD and ZP (1998)

x_4 : Road length per 100 square km of area (surfaced)

x_5 : Road length per 100 square km of area (unsurfaced)

x_6 : Commercial bank branches in districts (1999)

x_7 : Rate of expansion of commercial bank branches (1993–1999)

x_8 : Number of bank branches per lakh population

x_9 : Districtwise credit deposit ratio (March 1995–March 1999)

x_{10} : Per hectre availability of agricultural credit (1998–1999)

x_{11} : Villages electrified in West Bengal (1993–1998)

y : Per capita income in rupees (2000–01).

We get the following ranks of the districts according to infrastructure composite index (ICI)

Table 13.2: Rank of the Districts (Infrastructure)

District	*ICI*
Hoogly	1.510884
24 pgs (n)	0.867405
Darjiling	0.846306
Howrah	0.495655
Midnapur	0.403858
Jalpaiguri	0.337267
Burdwan	0.269468
24 pgs (s)	0.024033
Nadia	–0.23905
Bankura	–0.23936
Murshidabad	–0.37829
Purulia	–0.44377
Malda	–0.46442
Birbhum	–0.47196
Cooch Behar	–0.70832
Dinajpur (s)	–0.87018
Dinajpur (n)	–0.89707

From Table 13.2 we find that in the infrastructure front districts like Hoogly, 24 pgs (n), Darjiling, Howrah have high values of the composite index. Kolkata does not come into the picture because in Kolkata all roads are surfaced and PWD department does not maintain the roads.

In the manufacturing sector to identify the major factors influencing overall employment, the total output of the manufacturing sector in 1995-96 at 1980-91 prices (M) is regressed on total employment (EMP).We have chosen road length (RD) maintained by the (PWD) as a proxy for infrastructure and the number of commercial bank (CB) as a proxy for services. The regression results appear in endnotes (iii). As may be seen from regression results, since the observed value is less than the critical value, there is absence of any structural break in the manufacturing front also.

In the education front we consider certain selective indicators like number of primary, high and higher secondary schools, number of students per school, number of teachers, number of general degree colleges of the districts. We have compiled data from statistical abstract and HDR 2004 from these indicators.

x_1,x_2,x_3 : No. of primary,high and higher secondary schools (general education) 1998-1999

x_4,x_5,x_6 : No. of students per school in primary, high and higher secondary level 1998-1999

x_7,x_8,x_9 : No. of teachers in primary, high and higher secondary level 1998-1999

x_{10} : Districtwise no. of general degree colleges (1998)

y : Total Literacy (2001).

Table 13.3: Rank of the Districts (Education)

District	*ECI (Educational composite index)*
Midnapur	2.253862916
24 pgs (n)	1.517970822
Burdwan	0.682681495
24 pgs (s)	0.661678946
Hoogly	0.39367234
Murshidabad	0.068472937
Howrah	–0.067504147
Nadia	–0.102572403
Bankura	–0.254966723
Cooch Behar	–0.407347733
Jalpaiguri	–0.436601653
Birbhum	–0.525371343
Purulia	–0.533216214
Malda	–0.579932011
Darjiling	–0.785514028
Dinajpur (n)	–0.898810371
Dinajpur (s)	–0.985680012

Table 13.3 shows that Midnapur, 24 pgs. (n), Burdwan have high values of the educational composite index. Districts like Dinajpur (s & n), Darjiling, Malda exhibit poor performance. In the words of the Education Commission (1991) set up by the Govt. of West Bengal, "the most wide ranging changes since 1977 in the educational landscape in the state have been in the sphere of primary education". While establishing new primary schools in the state, attention is to be given on areas with predominance of marginalized section of the community. While in case of the primary schools, in Purulia number of students per school is the lowest; in case of junior/high school there are more schools in 24 parganas in relation to the enrolled students.

x_1	:	Access to toilets (% of household) 1991 census
x_2	:	Rural water supply (1998); no. of spot sources
x_3	:	Drinking water supply coverage of villages (percentage coverage) (1999)
x_4	:	Availability of doctors under state govt. health systems in blocks (no. of doctors per 1 lakh pop) (1999)
x_5,x_6,x_7,x_8	:	No. of beds available in medical college, district hospital, state general, and sub divisional level (1999)
x_9	:	Infant survival index (1999)
x_{10}	:	Percentage of safe delivery (1999).

Table 13.4: Rank of the Districts by Composite Index of the Health Sector

District	*SDCI*
Darjiling	5.356277632
Howrah	1.605421303
Burdwan	2.191020056
Bankura	1.564188765
Hoogly	.907712344
Purulia	.688539471
24 pgs (n)	–0.057046813
Birbhum	0.364498236
Nadia	–0.718852572
Jalpaiguri	–1.170562412
Dinajpur(s)	–1.412048367
Cooch Behar	–1.354366168
Dinajpur (n)	–1.612200753
Midnapur	–0.614105336
Malda	–1.888750873
24 pgs (s)	–1.737488531
Murshidabad	–1.856034387

From the composite index table (Table 13.4), we see that districts like Darjiling, Howrah, Burdwan have shown good performance in terms of development of health sector, whereas districts like Murshidabad, 24 pgs(s), Malda performed poorly in this regard.

Analysis of the Relative Position of the Districts Using All the Composite Indices

We will now study the overall ranking of the districts considering all the composite indices—social development composite index, agricultural composite index, infrastructure composite index, educational composite index (calculated from the previous tables) in Table 13.5. We also consider gender development index (collected from WBHDR; 2004) for measuring overall ranking of the districts. The component score coefficient matrix has been shown in Table 13.6.

Table 13.5: Aggregate Composite Indices

District	*SDCI*	*ACI*	*ICI*	*ECI*	*GDI**
Burdwan	2.191020056	1.37172273	0.269468	0.6826815	0.54
Birbhum	0.364498236	0.12174121	–0.4719631	–0.525371	0.42
Bankura	1.564188765	0.48271546	–0.2393592	–0.254967	0.46
Midnapur	–0.614105336	1.83451059	0.4038583	2.2538629	0.55
Howrah	1.605421303	–0.4639958	0.495655	–0.067504	0.56
Hoogly	0.907712344	1.05253001	1.5108838	0.3936723	0.56
24 pgs (n)	–0.057046813	0.29549489	0.867405	1.5179708	0.55
24 pgs (s)	–1.737488531	–0.4446169	0.0240328	0.6616789	0.51
Nadia	–0.718852572	0.1643218	–0.2390515	–0.102572	0.49
Murshidabad	–1.856034387	–0.0811003	–0.3782865	0.0684729	0.41
Dinajpur (n)	–1.612200753	–0.48069	–0.8970714	–0.89881	0.46
Dinajpur(s)	–1.412048367	–0.48069	–0.8701842	–0.98568	0.46
Malda	–1.888750873	–0.3886729	–0.4644241	–0.579932	0.39
Jalpaiguri	–1.170562412	–0.7508114	0.3372673	–0.436602	0.45
Darjiling	5.356277632	–1.219078	0.8463064	–0.785514	0.57
Cooch Behar	–1.354366168	–0.7403555	–0.7083203	–0.407348	0.45
Purulia	0.688539471	–0.7529666	–0.4437704	–0.533216	0.4

Source: SDCI, ACI, ICI, ECI calculated from previous tables

SDCI: Social Development Composite Index;

ACI: Agricultural Composite Index;

ICI: Infrastructure Composite Index;

ECI: Educational Composite Index;

GDI: Gender Development Index.

*GDI from Human Development Report, West Bengal, 2004.

Table 13.6: Component Score Coefficient Matrix

SDCI	0.18
ACI	0.235
ICI	0.307
ECI	0.27
GDI	0.312

SPSS 10.0 package is used to calculate the factor scores for the districts.

Extraction Method: Principal Component Analysis (The methodology appears in the appendix)

The ranking of the districts according to the aggregate score obtained from the above method is as follows:

Table 13.7: Aggregate Score

District	*AS*
Midnapur	1.3950385
Burdwan	1.3292691
Hoogly	1.3286256
24 pgs (n)	1.0897383
Darjiling	1.0820739
Howrah	0.6772368
Bankura	0.5391078
Nadia	0.1213988
24 pgs (s)	0.0936985
Birbhum	0.0675159
Purulia	–0.0848159
Jalpaiguri	–0.1146233
Murshidabad	–0.196571
Cooch Behar	–0.4614677
Malda	–0.4878931
Dinajpur (s)	–0.617091
Dinajpur (n)	–0.637918

The aggregate scores presented in Table 13.7 are more or less in conformity with the ranking of the districts according to HDI (WBHDR, 2004). The UNDP has suggested the use of Human Development Index (HDI) to capture the broad pattern of development in a region, which cannot be comprehended by the use of income criterion alone. The UNDP, in its attempt to construct the human development index, has considered three major dimensions of human development: (a) long and healthy life, as measured by life expectancy at birth; (b) knowledge, as measured by the adult literacy rate (with two-third weight) and the gross enrolment in primary, secondary and tertiary stage (with one third weight), and (c) a decent standard of living as measured by GDP per capita. Here DDP is used instead of GDP. The formula is

HDI = 1/3 (Infant survival index) + 1/3 (Education Index) + 1/3 (DDP index). The human development index thus calculated is given in Table 13.8:

Table 13.8: Human Development Index

District	*HDI VALUE*
24 pgs (n)	0.66
Darjiling	0.65
Burdwan	0.64
Hoogly	0.63
Midnapur	0.62
24 pgs (s)	0.60
Nadia	0.58
Jalpaiguri	0.53
Bankura	0.52
Cooch Behar	0.52
Dinajpur (n)	0.51
Dinajpur (s)	0.51
Birbhum	0.47
Murshidabad	0.46
Purulia	0.45
Malda	0.44

Source: HDR, 2004

Thus it is found that the ranking of the districts according to the aggregate score obtained from combining the composite indices by Principal Component Method, quite tallies with the ranking of the districts according to HDI index. Districts like Midnapur, Burdwan, Hoogly, 24 pgs, Darjiling, Howrah, are high rank holders in both the cases, whereas districts like Murshidabad, Malda, Purulia, Dinajpur, have less than the average score in both the cases.

4. Concluding Observation

In this study, we have tried to portray a comprehensive picture of the nature of the economy of West Bengal, which has been good in certain sectors while in others, the state has not made significant progress for the period under consideration. The study reveals that district development index is highly influenced by agricultural productivity, employment and infrastructure. The districts which have exhibited good performance, for example, in terms of agricultural composite index have not necessarily shown the same performance in other areas. Manufacturing output at the district level was found to be influenced by the level of employment. So emphasis must be given on employment generation programme. Districts like Midnapur, Darjiling, Burdwan, Hoogly, 24 pgs (n), Howrah, have shown fairly consistent high ranking in terms of all the composite indices. In this study we have often indicated the inadequacies of some data. So emphasis should be given in preserving such data and greater endeavor should be made in collection of more disaggregated level data. This paper, however, suggests that the growth of income is not adequate to bring about overall status of development of West Bengal. Expansion of social, infrastructure and human development with the help of Government, NGO and individual initiatives is also highly important in bringing about comprehensive development of the state of West Bengal.

Appendix

I. The compound growth rate of state domestic product (SDP)/per capita income (PCI) was calculated by using the following model.

$$\text{SDP (or PCI)} = AB^t$$

$$\text{Log SDP (or Log PCI)} = \text{Log } A + t \text{ Log } B$$

$$\text{sdp (pci)} = a + tb$$

Where t = time variable, sdp = Log SDP (or pci = Log PCI),

$a = \text{Log } A$, $b = \text{Log } B$

Compound growth rate (%) = (Antilog b –1)*100

The compound growth rates were calculated for the three periods, viz, 1980-81 to 1989-90, 1990-91 to 1999-00 and overall (1980-81 to 1999-00).

II. To construct ACI (Agricultural Composite Index), ICI (Infrastructural Composite Index), ECI (Educational Composite Index) and HCI (Health coposite index) for measuring the relative position of the districts in the state of West Bengal, a simple index of weighted standard score based on the each of the above indexes was prepared. For example ACI can be calculated as follows:

$$CI = \sum_{j=1}^{m} r_{oj} Z_{ij} \Big/ \sum_{j=1}^{m} r_{oj},$$

(i = 1,2,….18 districts j = 1,2,….m items)

CI = Weighted standard scores for agriculture

$Z_{ij} = (X_{ij} - X_{ij}) / S_{xij}$, the standard scores of the jth item in the ith district

X_{ij} and S_{xij}, are the mean and standard deviation

r_{0i} = correlation coefficient between agricultural productivity (dependent variable) and the jth item of independent variable (cropping intensity/ percentage of irrigated coverage/fertilizer consumption/ commercial bank branches/per hectare availability of agricultural credit/pucca road connectivity in villages/villages electrified/literacy rate/ livestock/agricultural tractor/sub-market yard).

III. Using the *Principal Component Analysis* (PCA) we find the aggregate score of each district on the basis of composite indices. PCA is a popular statistical technique used to convert multiple indicators to generate a one-dimensional indicator. It helps in contracting a large number of variables into a smaller number of indices so that the geographical units are made comparable. The composite index arrived at through PCA maximizes the sum of squares of correlation with the constituent variables. In PCA, linear combinations of the observed variables are formed which are orthogonal. The first principal component, the area of our study, is the combination that accounts for the largest amount of variance in the sample. Successive components explain progressively smaller portions of total sample variance. The factor matrix contains coefficients used to express a standardized variable in terms of factors. These coefficients are called factor loadings, since they indicate about how much weight is assigned to each factor. A factor can be estimated as a linear combination of the original variables. The method may be obtained as follows:

- We start by the simple correlation coefficient between the explanatory variables. These correlation coefficients may be arranged in a table, which we call correlation table. The correlation matrix is symmetrical, that is, the elements of each row are identical to the element of the corresponding column, since $r_{xi\,xj} = r_{xj\,xi}$
- We sum each column (or row) of the correlation table, obtaining k sums of simple

correlation coefficient $\sum_{j}^{k} r_{xi\,xj} = \sum_{i}^{k} r_{xj\,xi}$

- We compute the sum total of the column (or row) sums, i.e. $\sum_i^k \sum_j^k x_1 x_j$ and take its square root.
- Finally we obtain the loading (aij's) for the first principal component P1 by dividing each column (row) sum by the square root of the grand total.

  $a_{ij} = l_{ij} = \Sigma\, r_{xi\,xj} / (\Sigma\, \Sigma r_{xi\,xj})^{1/2}$

  where i refers to the ith variable x
- The sum of the squares of the loading of each principal component is called the latent root (or eigen value, or characteristic root) of two component and will be denoted by the greek letter λ with the subscript of the principal component to which it refers. The latent root of the first principal component P_1 is
- λ_1 (latent root of P_1) $= \Sigma \sum_i^k l_{11^2} + l_{12^2} + \ldots\ldots + l_{1k^2}$
- The percentage contribution of P_1 in the total variance of the standardized X's is defined by the expression λ_1/k *100 ,where k is equal to the number of X's (explanatory variable).

Endnotes

(i) The estimated regression equations are:

<u>1995-96:</u>

(PTY = 1407.74 –0.027 CI +10.62 IRG +0.00048 FC

(4.294) (-0.01) (2.85) (0.105)

R^2 = 0.563

$\overline{R}^2$ = 0.453

F = 5.147

RSS_1 = 1163802.3

No. of observations = 16

Degrees of freedom = 12

<u>2000-2001</u>

PTY = 1431.67 + 0.8298 CI +9.4153 IRG + 0.00188 FC

(5.198) (.5496) (4.7838) (1.1712)

R^2 = .7502

$\overline{R}^2$ = .6878

F = 12.013

RSS_2 = 430074.4

No. of observations = 16

Degrees of freedom = 12.

(ii) The pooled regression results are:

PTY = 1279.4369 + 1.192 CI + 9.34 IRG +.002 FC

(6.251) (.8919) (4.801) (1.191)

R^2 = .626

$\overline{R}^2$ = .586

RSS_P = 1838774.0

No. of observations = 32

Degrees of freedom = 28

Chow test # 1: the null hypothesis H_0 for the chow test # 1 is

$H_0: a_o = b_o, a_{CI} = b_{CI}, a_{IRG} = b_{IRG}, a_{FC} = b_{FC}$

$F_{K, n1+n2-2k} = ((RSS_P - (RSS_1+RSS_2))/K)/((RSS_1+RSS_2)/(n1+n2 - 2k)$

= .92195

The critical value of $F_{4,24}$ (0.01) = 4.22

(iii) Regression Results

<u>1995-96</u>

The estimated regression equation for the period 1995-96 is:

M = –943.86 + .084 EMP –4.518 RD M + 38.87 CB

(–.271) (5.436) (–0.675) (1.07)

R^2 = .941

$\overline{R}^2$ = .925

F = 58.211

RSS_1 = 3.11E+08

No. of observations = 15

Degrees of freedom = 11

<u>2000-2001</u>

The estimated regression equation for the period 2000-01

$$M = -7938.184 + 0.100\, EMP + 3.974 RD + 21.974\, CB$$
$$(-2.6) \quad (7.794) \quad (0.725) \quad (0.776)$$

R^2 = .970

$\overline{R}^2$ = .962

F = 115.086

RSS_2 = 2.45E + 08

No. of observations = 15

Degrees of freedom = 11

Pooled Regression Equation

$$M = -4678.24 + .09\, EMP - .774\, RD + 34.92\, CB$$
$$(-1.932) \quad (8.837) \quad (-.172) \quad (1.493)$$

R^2 = .944

$\overline{R}^2$ = .938

F = 146.77

RSS_P = 7.36E+08

No. of observations = 30

Degrees of freedom = 26

Chow test # 1 : the null hypothesis H_0 for the chow test # 1 is

$H_{0}: a_o = b_o, a_{EMP} = b_{EMP}, a_{RD} = b_{RD}, a_{CB} = b_{CB}$

$$F_{K,\, n1+n2-2k} = ((RSS_P - (RSS_1 + RSS_2))/K)/((RSS_1 + RSS_2)/(n1+n2-2k)$$
$$= 1.78057$$

The critical value of $F_{4,22}(0.05) = 2.82$

References

Chatterjee, B and D.K. Ghosh (2001) 'In search of a District Development Index' *State Institute of Panchayats and Rural Development,* Kalyani, West Bengal.

Dasgupta, S. (2004) 'West Bengal's Social Sectors—Challenges and Opportunities' in D. Mukhopadhayay (Edn.), Social Sectors of West Bengal: Concerns, Challenges and Opportunities, Department of Economics, St. Paul's C.M. College, Kolkata.

Dasgupta, P. (1993) *An Inquiry into Well-being and Destitution*, Oxford University Press.

Government of West Bengal (2002-03) '*Statistical Abstract*' Bureau of Applied Economics and Statistics.

Government of West Bengal, (2002-03) '*Economic Review*' Planning and Development Department.

Jana, S. and Mou, R. (2004) 'Human Development Index for the Districts of West Bengal, *Artha Beekshan,* June 2004.

Pal, D.P. and Jayanta S. (2003) 'Economic Development and Infrastructure: An Inter District Study in West Bengal', *Artha Beekshan,* June 2003

Pradhan, R.P. (2003) 'Agriculture Efficiency in Orissa: Problems and Prospects', *Journal of Rural Development*, NIRD, Hyderabad.

Singh, R. (2004) 'Rural Infrastructure Agricultural Development and Poverty in India: An Inter-State Study', *Journal of Rural Development*, NIRD, Hyderabad.

West Bengal Human Development Report (2004) Development and Planning Department, *Government of West Bengal*.

Theory, Policy and Actual Empirical Findings in India: Contrary to Mainstream Macroeconomic Perception—A Report

Prof. Rakshit* points out an important issue following the last observation of Mr. Ahluwalia regarding the connection between theory, policy and actual empirical findings. Mr. Ahluwalia has noted that during the global crisis India had a slowdown; our exports were badly hit and the government had to implement expansionary fiscal and monetary measures. After a year and a half, the economy recovered. However, the problem of development, Prof. Rakshit argues, is quite different. It is a long-term one and requires a different strategy. Again, the recovery after the crisis was marked by a curious feature. Though there was an increase in the level of aggregate production, most of the recovery took place in durable consumer goods industries, not so much in investment or non-durable consumer goods output. At the same time the turnaround was accompanied with sharp rises in food and agricultural prices. These features, Prof. Rakshit thinks, cannot be explained in terms of the mainstream theoretical framework. There are two things that may be noted in this connection. First, by far the most important source of stimulus was the substantial cuts in indirect taxes. This had little impact on food prices, but helped reducing prices of industrial products, especially of durable consumer goods. Again, given the inelastic demand for food items and their soaring prices, the less affluent consumers would not have enough income left to buy industrial goods which for these consumers consist mostly of non-durable products. The disparity in the growth rates of the two groups of products during recovery is thus not very difficult to discern.

Second, even though the source of inflation was purely supply-side and emanated from the food sector, no significant measure was taken to tackle the problem. The failure reflects the sway of conventional theory of inflation on the policy makers, even though it was largely irrelevant for the Indian economy. Hence arises the needs for identifying, in light of empirical evidence, the underlying economic mechanism at work and framing policies accordingly.

---

*Professor Mihir Kanti Rakshit, ICRA, made a comment on lecture delivered by Dr. Montek Singh Ahluwalia, Deputy Chairman Planning Commission of India, as the Chairperson of Inaugural session at the UGC sponsored Nation Conference of Centre for Economic Studies, Presidency University, Kolkata on August 28, 2010.

Conflicting Measure of Poverty and Inadequate Savings by the Poor—The Role of Status Driven Utility Function—A Report

Prof. Marjit* critically highlights the vital issues of his paper. Some of the important aspects of his discussions may be outlined in the following:

We are always conditioned by social status in our respective domain of operation and the utility function we assume in such a domain does contain the issue of relative social status. If, in absolute term, for example, someone gets some quantities of a good, and others gets the same good more, then the former gets disappointed; or if an individual has a black and white television or ambassador car and someone else has a color television or Mercedes, then the former may get dejected. Thus all these move towards the upsetting criteria. Even there is an egocentric trigger when we feel that we are better than someone. If we consider, for instance, the conferences or seminars of economists in international arena, each sort of pulling leg and ill grimace about the others lends credence to the fact that social status affects a person everywhere. This is an important issue, and so utility function should contain some arguments about the social status.

How does social status affect the consumption behavior of poor people if they actually become a bit richer? If an individual who is below poverty line (BPL) gets some money, he can move from BPL to APL. Then, instead of buying an extra glass of milk-which, it is assumed, he usually uses to drink- he would probably drink half of milk and use that extra money for buying potato chips or maybe even a small contrivance like cell phone. The implication is that it is not only the expenditure on nutritious good is going down but also the absolute amount of the commodity the individual is consuming is actually going down. We are here pointing towards inferior good. Conspicuous consumption is connected with the idea of relative social status and the latter may be biased towards the consumption of inferior good. In an excellent paper in the journal of social psychology Shivanathan and Pettit (2010) talk about

*Professor Sugata Marjit, Director, Centre for Studies in Social Science, Kolkata and R.B.I. Professor of Industrial Economics, presented his paper at the UGC sponsored National Level Conference of Centre for Economic Studies, Presidency University, Kolkata on August 30, 2010.

how people try to put extra weightage to conspicuous consumption. If someone gets afflicted for his poverty, he would, then, try to project himself upward, maybe, by buying top of the line. Through repeated experiments it is found that people try to put extra importance towards conspicuous consumption to rectify their image and to cast themselves upward. It implies that they are affected by relative social status. In their paper, Banerjee and Duflo (2006) highlight consumption behavior of the poor people in different countries: when poor people are actually becoming a bit richer they try to spend their income on things they should not spend on, and they do it very consistently across countries. Two important issues emerges out of these analyses: (i) poor people are not saving much, and (ii) poor people are spending a lot on conspicuous consumption.

Here we try to talk about, Prof. Marjit remarks, whether this kind of consumption behavior implies a diversion of resources to where it is actually spent on from where it should be spent on. Moav and Neeman (2010), in their paper titled 'Status and Poverty' published by Journal of European Economic Association, convey the idea of a world where capital market is imperfect: there is a difference between borrowing and lending rates, and there is a threshold level problem, i.e. one can't really accumulate human capital by financing on education so much if one is leaving something for posterity; then if he is spending too much money on conspicuous consumption, he will be ensnared into the poverty trap. So if a person has some money and does keep it for his children's education instead of buying, for example, mobile phones, only then will he be afforded to come out from the so called poverty trap and the next generation will not suffer. It, however, implies that if one allows relative social status to affect him then he wants to be richer which is not an unhealthy task; rather that may be a beneficial one. If people like to grow more, they would like to invest more, earn more and ultimately save more. That is not borne out from the empirical evidence that Banerjee and Duflo (2006) observed on different countries.

Hence the relevant issue might be, Marjit argues, whether the consumption behavior of poor people is a rational choice if he becomes a bit richer. He tries to examine this issue in a theoretical model. In this paper he uses utility function; but by transforming it a little bit he tries to show if he internalizes the behavioral assumptions made earlier, he will have two results from it. The first one is on the conflicting measures of poverty: a richer poor will actually be consuming less of nutritious goods than he or she would do rationally, and the second one would be the dynamic consequences (i.e. the saving behavior: how relative social status should have an impact on the savings behavior), which suggests that the more the richer poor consumes the luxury good, the intensity of his desire of consuming luxury good increases a lot; then he is nutritionally worse off, but economically he is better off. From the literature of relative social status and growth we also come to know, Marjit offer reasons, that as we are worried about our relative social status, we try to improve it more.

How does government promote for optimal taxation and subsidy policy when the welfare of the people is guided by relative social status? Basically optimal taxation would start, Marjit suggests, changing in this set-up and then the policies would depend on what people really think of welfare.

References

Banerjee, A.V. and E. Duflo (2006): 'Addressing Absence', *Journal of Economic Perspectives*, Vol. 20 (1), pp. 117–132.

Moav, O. and Z. Neeman (2010): 'Status and Poverty', *Journal of European Economic Association*, Vol. 8, No. 2-3, April-May, pp. 413–420.

Food Price Inflation in India—A Report

Prof. Abhirup Sarkar* talks about some vital issues which are affecting the people directly, especially the poorer section of the society. Some of the important issues may be delineated in the following:

Recently there has been a significant rise in the general price level and food prices particularly. Observing on the price indices, we will find lot of weightage on the food prices. A rise in food prices brings about a rise in the price indices. Whenever one talks about the inflation, the first thing that comes to mind is monetary policy. We were taught that inflation is a monetary phenomenon. If we do not have a sustained increase in money supply we cannot have inflation. Now here I think that monetary policy is not directly responsible for two reasons. First, inflation is calculated on point to point basis: what was the price, say, one year ago and what is the price now. Whenever there is a sudden price jump, immediately it shows up in inflation. But, more importantly, agricultural supplies come seasoned. If there is a crop failure, price would go up and stay at a higher level for almost a year. So if we calculate inflation on point to point basis, at each point we will get a higher inflation. We do not need a sustained increase in money supply to have inflation. Second reason is that the monetary policy is largely accommodating in the sense that if there is a rise in prices, there are channels through which money supply will automatically go up. If we look at classification of bank credits done by the Reserve Bank of India, there are non-food credits and food credits. Food credit is very important in the context of Indian Economy. Basically, food credits are the credit advanced to various agencies and individuals for holding food grains. If there is a rise in the prices of food grains, then bank credits would naturally go up if you do not restrict food credits. And that would create more money. In that sense, money supply has been accommodated. So I won't look at monetary phenomenon to explain expansion, rather we will look at the real phenomenon which is causing this inflation—especially food price inflation.

Now, we will broadly talk about supply side factors and demand side factors. What are the supply side factors? One can also make a distinction

---

*Prof. Abhirup Sarkar, Professor of Economics, Indian Statistical Institute, Kolkata, presented his paper at the UGC sponsored National Level Conference of Centre for Economic Studies, Presidency University, Kolkata on August 30, 2010.

between short run and long run factors. In the year before last year the growth rate of food grain was negative, i.e., total supply went down. The supply that we are consuming now experienced a negative growth which means that total amount available in the economy went down. Therefore the food supply immediately caused raising the prices of food products. This is the short run factor. In the long run, it can be seen that from 1999 onwards if you look at the growth rate of food grains it was about 1.2% whereas the rate of population growth has been 1.4% for the economy as a whole. So there has been a sectoral decline in the per capita availability of food grains, and as a result the food prices rose. If we look at the NSS figures, we find that the supply of food grains has indeed gone down and thereby the per capita consumption of food grains has declined. So it must be the supply side shock which led to reduction in supply and therefore rise in food prices. One can often add other factors. Often it is said that food price inflation is due to speculative apprehension. We can try to understand whether speculation can play a role. The standard argument for speculation is that if people expect prices of food grains to go up in future then they will try to accumulate stocks now. Stock building will lead to withdrawal of supply leading to rise in the prices. You can think of a speculative bubble in the sense that own price goes up, and people might expect the prices to rise further and so on.

The next result of speculation is that of hoarding. When people expect the prices of the food grain to rise in future, they buy huge amounts of food grains at the lower price and store it to create stock. Thus there is again a withdrawal of supply from the market and price of food grain rises. The fact is that despite considerable increase for the stock of food grains during the very recent years, the price of food grains significantly increases. The additional factors that may bring about food price inflation includes the government's inefficiency to fight against inflation. These are, among others, government's food procurement and release, FCI's stock management and lobbying.

Next comes the demand side factors. The National Rural Employment Guarantee Act provides a legislative act which aims at ensuring hundred days of wage employment to rural households whose adult members volunteer to do unskilled manual work. This scheme has brought about an increase in the purchasing power of the rural sector. This has lead to an increased demand for food from the poorer section of the society. With the rise in population there has been a substantial rise in demand for food from the aggregated society. Thus comes the problem of inadequate supply to the rising demand for food.

In the long run food security also poses certain problems. The serious problem of inefficient agricultural production and scarcity of land as a factor of production with exploding increase in population is very difficult to solve. The problem also rises day-by-day due to this increase in population. Again, though there has been a substantial rise in the income status of the people in general, the real purchasing power of the people has gone down due to rise in price level and inflationary pressure. Thus the lower purchasing power creates impediment in the supply-demand equilibrium.

How is it possible to increase the real purchasing power of the people? One might say that it can be created presumably through industrialization. But the implementation faces constraints. For the development of industries and infrastructure, more and more of land is required to support them. Similarly, the requirement of this scarce natural resource also rises in the agricultural sector to boost agricultural productivity through making better irrigation channels and dams which also need land. Both these issues would reduce the availability of land for the agricultural production, thus lowering per capita output and, in effect, causes price rising.

The problem also grows due to the fact that the stock of food holding by the government, known as buffer stock, is inefficiently utilized by the government. The creation of the buffer stock and inefficient utilization of the same creates further shortage in the supply of food grains thus raising the prices.

How inefficient is the distribution of food grains per capita in India during the current years? In India acreage of land is high, productivity is low; but per capita food grains production is considerably high. Significantly, higher per capita production does not guarantee higher per capita consumption reflecting that high per capita production is beset with high level of poverty. The fact is that in states like Madhya Pradesh, Chhattisgarh, Orissa, Uttarakhand, West Bengal have much higher per capita production, but they are beset with much higher level of poverty. It lends credence to the fact of inefficient distributional system of the country.

Index

T

U

V

www.ingramcontent.com/pod-product-compliance
Lightning Source LLC
Chambersburg PA
CBHW071339230926
51846CB00002B/387
* 9 7 8 8 1 8 4 2 4 6 7 7 3 *